The Real Mary

Why Evangelical Christians Can Embrace the Mother of Jesus

Scot McKnight

PARACLETE PRESS
BREWSTER, MASSACHUSETTS

The Real Mary: Why Evangelical Christians Can Embrace the Mother of Jesus

2007   First Printing

Copyright © 2007 by Scot McKnight

ISBN 10: 1-55725-523-7
ISBN 13: 978-1-55725-523-5

Scripture quotations are taken from the Holy Bible, Today's New International Version™ TNIV® Copyright © 2001, 2005 by International Bible Society®. All rights reserved worldwide.

Excerpt from "Journey of the Magi" in COLLECTED POEMS 1909-1962 by T.S. Eliot, copyright 1936 by Harcourt, Inc., and renewed 1964 by T.S. Eliot, reprinted by permission of the publisher.

Library of Congress Cataloging -in- Publication
McKnight, Scot.
  The real Mary : why Evangelical Christians can embrace the Mother of Jesus / by Scot McKnight.
      p. cm.
  ISBN-13: 978-1-55725-523-5
  1. Mary, Blessed Virgin, Saint—Theology. 2. Bible. N.T. Gospels—Criticism, interpretation, etc. I. Title.
  BT613.M43 2007
  232.91—dc22
                                                          2006029126
10 9 8 7 6 5 4 3 2 1

Published by Paraclete Press
Brewster, Massachusetts
www.paracletepress.com
Printed in the United States of America

Contents

Part II
The Ongoing Life of Mary in the Church

Part III
Embracing the Real Mary

Forgive us, gentle maiden, if we learnt to give you
Less respect than heaven would have wished;
For we fell in love with the Son of your great love,
So as not to venerate you more than Him.
 from "Wales and the Virgin Mary"
                    JOHN GWILI JENKINS

. . . were we led all that way for
Birth or Death? There was a Birth, certainly,
We had evidence and no doubt. I had seen birth and death,
But had thought they were different; this Birth was
Hard and bitter agony for us, like Death, our death.
We returned to our places, these Kingdoms,
But no longer at ease here, in the old dispensation,
With an alien people clutching their gods.
I should be glad of another death.
 from "The Journey of the Magi"
                    T.S. ELIOT

part I
The Real Mary of the Gospels

1
Why a Book about the Real Mary?

"Why are you—a Protestant—writing a book about Mary?" I've been asked this question many times. In fact, one person asked me the following question: "Wasn't Mary a Roman Catholic?" (No kidding.)

Why write a book for Protestants about Mary? Here's why:

Because the story about the real Mary has never been told. The Mary of the Bible has been hijacked by theological controversies whereby she has become a Rorschach inkblot in which theologians find whatever they *wish* to find. In the midst of this controversy, the real Mary has been left behind. It is time to let her story be told again. Over the past ten years I have read shelves of books and articles about Mary, and I have discovered that almost no one is interested in what the real Mary was like in her day. *The Real Mary* attempts to fill in that gap and underscore the real Mary.

Why a book about Mary?

Because while Mary's story is that of an ordinary woman, it also the story of a woman with an extraordinary vocation (being mother to the Messiah) who learned to follow this Messiah Jesus through the ordinary struggles that humans face. In this sense, Mary represents each of us—both you and me—in our call to follow Jesus.

Why a book about Mary?

Because for years the view of Mary in the Church has been made unreal. Mary has become for many little more than a compliant "resting womb" for God, and she has become a stereotype of passivity in the face of challenge, of self-sacrifice at the expense of one's soul care, and of quietude to the point of hiding in the shadows of others. Nora O. Lozana-Diaz, a professor at the Hispanic Baptist Theological College, traces the influence of what she calls *marianismo* on Latin culture and claims this false view of Mary (*marianismo*) oppresses women instead of challenging them to live with courage before God—as Mary herself did! If a false view damages all of us, a more accurate view can encourage all of us, women and men.

Why write a book about Mary?

Because she was the mother of Jesus, and being the mother of Jesus ought to matter to each of us.

Because the Magnificat, her song in Luke's first chapter, is the *Magna Carta* of early Christian songs and a mosaic of what God would do when Jesus, the Messiah, came: "My soul magnifies the Lord and my spirit rejoices in God my Savior, for he has been mindful of the humble state of his servant." And these are just the opening lines of her song.

Why write a book about Mary?

Because the developments about Mary in the Roman Catholic and Eastern Orthodox traditions have generated "reaction formation." Many of us Protestants have reacted against Mary so much we have been formed now in such a way that Mary has been pushed entirely off the stage. Most of us know far more about what we *don't* believe about Mary—that she wasn't immaculately conceived, that she had other children with Joseph and wasn't perpetually virgin, etc.—than what we *do* believe about Mary.

Why write a book about Mary?

Because a book about Mary for evangelicals that focuses on the real Mary, so far as I know, has never been written. Other books have engaged in polemics about the immaculate conception, her perpetual virginity, devotion to Mary, and other so-called Marian dogmas. But, to my knowledge, no one has written a book about the life and character of Mary helping us develop a positive, Protestant view of Mary. Allow me to say this more forcibly: We are Protestants; we believe in the Bible; Mary is in the Bible; we need to believe what the Bible says about Mary. *The Real Mary* is designed to speak to our tradition.

Why write a book about Mary?

Because the Cold War between Protestants and Roman Catholics over Mary has ended. There are many reasons for this, some political, some social, some theological, and some global, but evangelical Presbyterian pastor Mark Roberts of

Irvine, California, thinks at least one reason the Cold War has ended is the song "Mary Did You Know?" Written decades ago by Mary Lowry and now recorded by more than thirty Christian artists, this song leads us back to the kind of Mary—the real Mary—that Protestants can embrace.

I have one final answer to the question "Why write a book about Mary?"

Because the real Mary always leads us to Jesus. When we discover the real Mary, the one who lived in first-century Galilee with Joseph, who I believe nurtured other children, and who struggled at times herself, we also discover someone we can embrace because Mary embraced her son as we are called to do. When you find the real Mary of Scripture, the Mary of the first century, you'll discover that she'll be talking about Jesus and pointing us all to Jesus.

2
"May it be"
WOMAN OF FAITH

The first Christmas was full of surprises. Mary was a young, poor, Jewish woman from an obscure Jewish village called Nazareth when the angel Gabriel startled her. Perhaps she was sleeping and the news came in a dream; perhaps she was in a room praying all alone; perhaps she was meditating by a stream of water. Somewhere, somehow, the angel appeared and brought out from under his wings a special envelope with the heavenly news that Mary had been chosen by God to be the mother of a son.

Gabriel informed her that her son was not going to be just any son, like a Jacob or a Reuben or a Benjamin. No, her son would be the Son of the Most High, the Davidic king of Israel, the long-awaited Messiah. And even more surprising to Mary was that she would conceive miraculously: God's powerful Spirit, that Spirit who brooded over the waters on Earth's Opening Day, would brood over her and create a miracle in her womb.

An angel for a visitor, news that she'd have a baby son, and the word that her son would be the Messiah: Surely, Mary was surprised. *But the biggest surprise was that Mary consented to God's plan.* After Gabriel read to her God's good news, Mary consented with the simple spoken words "may it be" (Luke 1:38).

We have two things working against us as Protestants when it comes to understanding statements like "may it be" by Mary: We have not only generally ignored her, but we have also stereotyped Mary as a Christmas figure. Let's look again at the events that led up to that first Christmas, for in so doing not only will we see the wonder of her statements but also we will find standing there the real Mary.

However surprising and joyous that day must have been, when Mary whispered "may it be" to the angel Gabriel, the inner seams of Mary's life were ripped apart. We need to remember that Mary's "may it be" to Gabriel occurred months before her "I do" to Joseph. On that day Mary heard the strange news from God that she would conceive out of wedlock as part of God's plan. For an engaged Jewish woman, that would have been a great surprise; that's not how God or Jewish law worked. And it's not how society worked either.

To be a Jewish woman and pregnant before marriage meant that many would question the integrity of her "I do" to Joseph. Sooner or later, the wagging tongues would have been claiming that they'd eventually find out who had been with Mary. That was Mary's real world.

In that same real world, Mary's "may it be" was an act of courageous faith. We take Mary's act of consenting to the angel's words for granted. We need to consider her context—what it have been like for a first-century teenage Jewish woman to trust God and what it would have been like to tell this conception story first to her family and then to Joseph and then to others in public. And when we consider this context, we will come into touch with Mary's real faith. We can romanticize her faith and we can idealize her example and we can stiffen her up by standing her up in a Christmas crèche, but we can't get away from the stubborn reality that a young woman pregnant before marriage would have a questionable and spreading reputation—however false the accusations.

Mary's faith in a Torah world

Mary knew what the facts about her life would point toward, and she knew the sort of things that would be said about her on street corners in backwater Nazareth.

Mary was *young*. Most sources suggest she was about thirteen, though some would raise her age to sixteen. Mary was also *engaged*. It would be some months before she and Joseph had their wedding ceremony. Even though only engaged, they were legally husband and wife except for sexual relations. In Mary's Torah world, from the moment of betrothal and not from the moment of the wedding ceremony (as is the case in the Western world), Joseph and Mary were considered husband and wife. She was young and she was engaged, but the hard fact for Mary was that she was already pregnant.

Mary was *pregnant*, and because it is clear from every reading of the Gospels that Joseph knew that he was not the father, her status was also immediately clear: She would have been labeled an adulteress, as she made no claim to having been forcibly violated.

Joseph, now her husband according to the Torah, was not the father; there must have been another man, adding up to a legal accuration of adultery. Once again according to the Torah, because Joseph and Mary were legally husband and wife, any sexual behavior on Mary's part outside that relationship would have been considered adultery (rather than fornication—in which case another law applied).

The Torah, which regulated Mary's society and her own life, stated this about adultery: *death by stoning for adultery*. Here are the words from Deuteronomy 22:23–24:

> If a man happens to meet in a town a virgin pledged to be married and he sleeps with her, you shall take both of them to the gate of that town and stone them to death— the young woman because she was in a town and did not scream for help, and the man because he violated another man's wife. You must purge the evil from among you.

Because life is frequently complex, there were issues and evidence to consider for those whose task it was to administer such laws: How do you know if the woman really is guilty of adultery? What if she claimed she had been raped? What if her husband had brought false charges against her? What if the young woman denied any wrongdoing? In the midst of all the village gossip, there was a practical, legal question:

How to determine if a woman was guilty of adultery in disputable cases?

The law of "bitter waters" was designed for disputable cases. According to the fifth chapter of Numbers, a suspected adulteress (*sotah*) was brought before the priest, required to let her hair hang down and under oath asked to drink the bitter waters: a mixture of dust, holy water, and the ink of the priest's written curse. The oath involved these words: "may the LORD cause you to become a curse among your people when he makes your womb to miscarry and your abdomen swell." If the woman was guilty, she would become sick. If she didn't become sick, she was acquitted.

Whatever we might think today, this law was implemented in the ancient world. And by the first century this legal procedure of drinking bitter waters sometimes became a public display of justice and other times outright family revenge. In the first century, so far as we can tell from later rabbinic sources, the *sotah*, or suspected adulteress, was brought into the court in Jerusalem to see if a confession could be extracted. If the *sotah*—suspected adulteress—maintained her innocence, which Mary would have maintained, she would have been taken to a conspicuous location (such as Nicanor's Gate) for public humiliation. She would have been required to drink the bitter waters, her clothes would have been torn enough to expose a breast, her hair would have been let down, and all her jewelry would have been removed. And passersby, especially women, would have been encouraged to stare at the publicly shamed woman in order to make an object lesson of her.

That is the real world of a suspected adulteress. That is also the real world of Mary.

Mary's faith as "may it be"

What was it like for Mary to have said "may it be" in that sort of world? Here are the sorts of things that would have torn through Mary's mind the minute Gabriel explained to her this "good news." Instantaneously—because she grew up in a Torah world—Mary's mind would have connected her pregnancy to being a *sotah* (suspected adulteress) and to the public humiliation of a trial, and to how Joseph, her Torah-observant husband, would respond. We, as those who are familiar with the story, already know that Joseph never went forward with the "bitter waters" procedure, yet that is what *we* know. With the scent of the angel still in Mary's presence, she had little idea how Joseph might respond to her claim of a virginal conception. What were the chances that her Torah-observant husband would back down from insisting that legal procedures be followed? Slim.

There's more to what Mary instantaneously knew, and most of these things we have learned from Jewish sources at the time of Jesus. She knew that villagers would taunt and ostracize her son. He'd hear the accusation that he was an illegitimate child (in Hebrew, a *mamzer*) and that he would be prohibited from special assemblies (Deut. 23:2). She knew as well that Joseph's reputation as an observant Jew would have been called into question. As we noted in the law about stoning the adulteress, she knew that he was legally required to divorce her. And one more mental connection for Mary was that he could leave her stranded with the Messiah-to-be without a father. She knew that they were poor and that any legal settlement that came to her after the divorce would make life financially difficult. No sane, intelligent, pious young Jewish woman—and Mary was all these things and more—could avoid thinking these very things about herself, about Jesus, and about Joseph.

She must have wondered if there was an easier way.

Knowing what the Torah said, knowing how that law was interpreted, and knowing what her society would accuse her of, we are ready to be surprised (if not amazed) that Mary consented to Gabriel with the simple words "may it be" as recorded in Luke's Gospel (1:38).

Why then, we ask, did Mary consent to this plan? Because she knew God. She knew from the pages of her people's history that the God of Israel was a merciful God who would look after her. She knew the stories about other women who were threatened in Jewish history who were protected by God—women whose stories are found in the Bible, women like Tamar, Rahab, Ruth, and Bathsheba, women whom the evangelist Matthew singles out when he writes his genealogy that leads to Joseph, Mary, and Jesus. Because of Mary's trust in God, and in spite of all these threatening thoughts of accusation and rebuke, Mary uttered those courageous words that changed history: "I am the Lord's servant. *May it be* to me according to your word."

Mary, in faith, consented to God's plan. Mary, in faith, began to carry a cross before Jesus was born. Mary began to suffer for the Messiah before the Messiah suffered.

Mary would never have a normal life again. Mary's family, Mary's friends, and Mary's Nazareth would never look at her the same again. If later evidence is any indication, very few would believe her story. I was stunned the first time I read these words about Mary from the great reformer Martin Luther:

> How many came in contact with her, talked, and ate and drank with her, who perhaps despised her and counted her but a common, poor, and simple village maiden, and who, had they known, would have fled from her in terror?

Walking around Galilee was a young and special woman who seemed to be ready for the extraordinary vocation God had called her to perform. But surely we will ask: How was Mary so prepared? The answer to that question can be found by looking at Mary's Song, called the Magnificat, found in Luke 1:46–55. When we listen carefully to that song of Mary's, we'll understand both why she was ready and also why we must contend that Mary was a woman of deep and courageous faith.

3

"He has brought down rulers"

WOMAN OF JUSTICE

In the 1980s the government of Guatemala banned any public reciting of Mary's Magnificat because it was deemed politically subversive. The Magnificat banned? For being subversive? That gentle Mary's Song subversive? Yes, indeed—the song surprises many of us. If, as if for the first time, we read the Magnificat with the call for justice in mind, we may find ourselves sympathizing with those who think it subverts injustice.

In countries whose citizens lack the basic liberties to say what they think, worship as they want, and to acquire basic needs, a bold plea for justice is an act of subversion. Mary made her bold plea in song. Not long after Mary sang this song, Magi from the East informed Herod, the cruel king of Israel, that a recent newborn would become king. Herod's response was to slaughter all the innocent children two years old and younger in the village of Bethlehem. If Herod thought the mere news of a baby boy in Bethlehem was subversive, what do you think he thought when he heard the words (or ideas) found in Mary's song? If we read Mary's song in Mary's real world, we will see that it is a song about turning injustices inside out and power upside down.

Mary's Song—the Magnificat—is more than a pious canticle sung in liturgical churches throughout the world every evening at Vespers to celebrate personal faith. Much more than this, Mary's song praises God for cracking the heavens wide open and descending into the world to establish justice and rout unjust rulers.

Mary's Song (in Herod's world)

As soon as the angel Gabriel left Mary, she hurried down to the home of her older relative, Elizabeth, to share the good news. Mary knew that Elizabeth, an aging barren wife of a priest, also had been visited by God, and that she, too, would give birth to a special son. As soon as Mary crossed the threshold, Elizabeth herself burst into a poetic blessing for Mary. Then Mary echoed back with what God was doing in her own womb. Here are the first lines of Mary's Magnificat, now found in Luke's first chapter. (We call this song the Magnificat because the first line in the Latin translation is *Magnificat anima mea Dominum*, or literally "Glorifies / my soul / the Lord.")

My soul glorifies the Lord
and my spirit rejoices in God my Savior . . .

Why does Mary break into song? Because not only is God giving to her a son, but also this miracle son will become the Davidic king and establish a new Davidic dynasty in Jerusalem that will last forever and ever. Remember that in Luke's first chapter when Gabriel visited Mary he told her that her son would be "great" and would be called the "Son of the Most High," that God would give her son "the throne of his father David," and that his "kingdom would never end." Mary understood Gabriel's words as the fulfillment of God's promise to David generations before—recorded for us in 2 Samuel's seventh chapter.

Knowing that her son will be the Davidic king and knowing that God has chosen to bring that king into the world through her womb, Mary explains why she needs to "magnificate"—why she needs to express her gratitude in song:

> *for he has been mindful*
> *of the humble state of his servant.*
> *From now on all generations will call me blessed,*
> *for the Mighty One has done great things for me—*
> *holy is his name.*

Mary's next words form an announcement, a voice from the bottom of society, that justice has finally arrived. This means the powers are being subverted. For others sitting with her at the margins of society, her words could only mean that Herod the Great, king of Israel, who had had his own family members assassinated and who had taxed Israel well beyond her means, would be overthrown. Read these words with one of your eyes on that petty tyrant Herod:

> *[God's] mercy extends to those who fear him,*
>> *from generation to generation.*
> *He has performed mighty deeds with his arm;*
> *he has scattered those who are proud in their inmost thoughts.*
> *He has brought down rulers from their thrones*
>> *but has lifted up the humble.*
> *He has filled the hungry with good things*
>> *but has sent the rich away empty.*
> *He has helped his servant Israel,*
>> *remembering to be merciful*
>>> *to Abraham and his descendants forever,*
>>>> *just as he promised our ancestors.*

When Mary declared that God "has brought down rulers from their thrones," anyone listening at the time would have heard implications for Herod the Great and Rome. When she announced that God has "sent the rich away empty," hearers would have immediately thought of Herod the Great and those benefiting from heavy taxation. When she proclaimed that God "has lifted up the humble" and "has filled the hungry with good things," Mary's listeners would have turned their attention to poor people like Mary herself. Had Mary sung this song in Nazareth among the peasants they would have all hoisted a toast and shouted "Hallelujah!" and "Amen!"

Herod's days of taxing Israel, flaunting her laws, and dotting Israel's landscape with pagan shrines were numbered. Mary was already announcing justice as fact.

The Magnificat was for Mary's world what "We Shall Overcome" was to the African American community in the USA in the 1960s and 1970s. I recall in 1970 sitting in an all-school assembly at my high school when African American students gathered together to sing this song: It was both scary and exciting all at once. There was a steely protest as well as a determination to put away social injustices when those students sang in a confident faith these words:

We shall overcome,
we shall walk hand in hand,
we shall all be free,
we are not afraid,
we are not alone,
the whole wide world around,
we shall overcome.

Mary's Magnificat was *that* kind of song. You can chant Mary's Song at Vespers or you can sing it aloud during Advent, but don't forget that its powerful words give one the sense of a rally and a revival more than the planned Scripture reading of the pious.

Mary's Character

If this is what Mary's song was really like, the image we have of Mary needs an upgrade. We need a Real Mary 2.0. When we think of Mary, the first thing that *should* come to mind is the kind of courage we find among informed protesters—and, by reading the Magnificat in context, we can imagine Mary to be wiry and spirited and resolved and bold and gutsy. Maybe we should call her the Blessed *Valorous* Mary instead of the Blessed Virgin Mary. Some think of her as tender; we might instead think of her as tenacious. Some think of her song as a splendid piece of spirituality that could be tucked away in a pew hymnal, but her song belongs instead on the shelf with socio-spiritual songs of protest against unjust rulers.

Mary was indeed holy and pious and humble—this all comes into play when Mary said "may it be." And the Magnificat expresses a profound sense of God's work for God's glory. But that servant girl of God had more than simple exemplary personal piety. Mary, if we learn to see what she was like through the Magnificat in Herod's world, was a tiger waiting to pounce on the moment when God's Messiah would be set loose. This woman of faith longed for the day when Herod the Great would meet a just end and God would appoint a true Davidic king—as 2 Samuel 7 predicted—and reestablish forever the Davidic dynasty in Jerusalem. God's news through Gabriel, that her son would become the Davidic king, was the particular hope that she and many others most wanted.

"What took you so long?" Mary must have asked God.

Mary's God

Sometimes we miss the fact that God is omnipresent in Mary's song. Here is a list of what Mary was inspired to say about God, who was invading the Land to strip away injustice and at the same time to restore God's people to mercy, peace, and justice.

The *Mighty One* has done great things for me.

Holy is *his* name.

His mercy extends to those who fear him.

He has performed mighty deeds with his arm.

He has scattered those who are proud.

He has brought down rulers from their thrones.

He has lifted up the humble.
He has filled the hungry with good things.
He has sent the rich away empty.
He has helped his servant Israel.
He has remembered to be merciful.

God is mighty, God is holy, and this God is also (unlike Herod) merciful. So confident was Mary's faith in God's promise through Gabriel that she put all these lines in the *past tense!* The conception was just a few days behind her but her conviction was that *God's promise was as good as done.* Herod's days are numbered. The days of a new Davidic dynasty have arrived!

Mary believed that God was about to turn the table of justice right side up.

Mary's Vision, Isaiah's Vision

Mary's Magnificat, if we think of it being sung during Herod's political and social reign (which we usually don't do), can be summarized in words like these: "Herod *de*throned and Jesus *en*throned!" As the life of Mary's faith unfolds in the Gospels, we will learn that these graphic hopes to dethrone Herod and enthrone Jesus will give way to a more refined understanding of what the title "Messiah" means. However, at this point in her life, Mary clearly envisioned an earthly Davidic dynasty with Jesus sitting on the throne in Jerusalem.

How could the real Mary not have thought like this at this point in her life? Isaiah's eleventh chapter was at the center of what Jews thought of the Messianic kingdom. Here are some of its earthy, graphic lines:

A shoot will come up from the stump of Jesse
  [a Davidic ancestor].
     The Spirit of the Lord will rest on him.
     With righteousness he will judge the needy,
        with justice he will give decisions for the poor.
     With the breath of his lips he will slay the wicked.
     The wolf will live with the lamb.
     For all the earth will be filled with the knowledge
        of the LORD.
     The nations will rally to him.
     He will . . . gather the exiles of Israel.

What words come to mind for the Davidic kingdom? Messiah, Spirit of God, justice for the needy and poor, judgment for the wicked, peace throughout all of creation, salvation for all, and Israel's lost tribes will find their way home.

This is what Mary thought. Her hopes were subversive.

Notice how similar Mary's words are to Isaiah's and notice also how concrete her images are:

     [God] is merciful to those who fear him.
     He will scatter the proud.
     He will bring down rulers.
     He will lift up the humble.
     He will fill the hungry.
     He will send the rich away empty.

If you were a first-century poor woman, if you were hungry and oppressed, if you had experienced the injustices of Herod the Great, and if you stood up in Jerusalem and announced that the proud and the rulers and the rich would be yanked down from their high places, it is likely you'd be tried for treason and put to death for disturbing the "peace."

If you were Herod or one of his twelve wives or one of his many sons with hopes of the throne, you would have heard these words as an act of protest, if not revolution or rebellion. Even if you, as Mary, were to argue with your accusers that these are words straight out of the Bible, you'd be accused of subversion, of wanting your son to become the next king. You just might end up crucified.

Which was exactly what did happen to her son, and the reason Jesus was crucified was that he took the same stands against similar oppressive leaders and that he promised the same kind of revolution to the poor and needy. The Spirit who inspired Jesus was the same Spirit who inspired Mary's Song of protest.

Now, if we look again at our Christmas crèches or at paintings and artwork of Mary, do those reminders of the first Christmas tell the real Mary's story? Do they tell us of a courageous woman who went toe-to-toe with Herod the Great over matters of everyday concern? Do these reminders suggest themes that when Jesus made them his own would get him crucified? Have we tamed Mary into the passive, pious mother of Jesus?

If we have, we need a real version of Mary.

As the real Mary's own life unfolds in what follows, we see that her hope for a Davidic dynasty with her son on the throne will undergo a major shift—not unlike the shift that all of Jesus' disciples will experience. But at this point in her young life, Mary's heart clings to Israel's hope for a Davidic Messiah who would replace Herod. It would be unfair to Mary to expect her to have any other kind of hope; that was what everyone in the Jewish world expected.

we give away and receive at Christmas. And, third, we note the somber, sober, white-faced, emotionless image we discover in the history of Christian art about Mary. Add these up, and you get a "nice" young Mary. This is what most of us think about Mary.

I admit that I am disturbed by those somber-faced statues of Mary draped in a Carolina-blue robe and by those seemingly emotionless, white-faced icons found in some European churches showing Marys with bleeding hearts extending out of her chest.

Here's why those statues bother me: Because the Mary of the Bible is never portrayed as somber-faced or emotionless. Mary was a muscular, wiry woman whose eyes were aglow with a dazzling hope for justice and whose body evoked a robust confidence in the God who was about to turn the world upside down through her son.

We've seen that Mary was a courageous young woman of faith willing to announce that the days of Herod were numbered. We are about to see that Mary's courageous faith would prove a threat to a Caesar Augustus as well. To see this, we have to look at the "gospel" that was proclaimed in Rome.

The gospel of Rome

Who was Augustus? To see his significance, we need to realize that Rome's history is neatly divided into the period of the Republic (510 BC to 27 BC) and the Principate (27 BC to AD 284). The man who turned Rome from the Republic to the Principate (or, the Roman Empire) was Caesar Augustus. Augustus had been adopted by the dictator Julius Caesar. After his death, Julius Caesar was officially declared to be a god, and from that time on Augustus was considered "son of god." When Augustus seized power in Rome, he ended the bitter civil wars and created what is now called the *pax Romana*, the peace of Rome. Because he brought peace to Rome, Augustus was its savior. The rise of Augustus was declared throughout the Roman Empire as *"good news"* (or "gospel").

The gospel story out of Rome was this: Caesar Augustus, son of god, our savior, has brought peace to the whole world.

The gospel of the angels

It can't be accidental that the four words that expressed the gospel of the Roman Empire are the same four words the angels used to express the gospel about Jesus. The gospel that the angels announced to Mary and to the shepherds was the good news that Jesus, the Son of God, was the Savior. That could only mean one thing: Caesar Augustus was not. That's dangerous.

When Gabriel swooshed into Mary's life, he informed her that "the holy one to be born will be called the *Son of God*." Nine months later, when Jesus was born, angels appeared to shepherds near Bethlehem and used terms about Jesus, the Messiah, that indicated that Jesus' birth was a threat to Augustus. "Do not be afraid," the angel said to the shepherds. "I bring you *good news* [or "the gospel"] of great joy that will be for all the people." The angel was speaking here of Jesus, the one who would bring the true gospel. "Today in the town of David," the angel proceeds to declare, "a *Savior* has been born to you; he is the Messiah, the Lord." And then we hear from a chorus of angels these words about what Jesus will bring: "Glory to God in the highest heaven, and on earth *peace* to those on whom his favor rests." The shepherds heard these words from the angels—and they told these words to Mary.

There is no question, then, about the danger Mary presented to the world. She knew this new gospel story, a gospel story that blatantly countered the gospel of Rome. Mary's son would be a challenge to Rome's gospel because it would be her son, the true Son of God and the true Savior of the world, who would bring the true gospel of peace for the world.

The gospel of Mary

Mary was in the middle of these announcements. We cannot doubt that when she heard these words from the angel and the shepherds she added it all up and came to one natural conclusion. The conclusion is that she was suddenly caught in the dangerous story of two kings who would somehow come into conflict.

Rome used four expressions for Augustus, the angels used the same four expressions for Jesus, but it was Mary who began to tell the story that became our Gospels. We owe more to Mary than many of us think. The real Mary is the first voice behind the Gospels we now read, and that first voice made her a dangerous woman.

Mary pondering a dangerous story

Here's what we have to consider anew: The gospel of Jesus was a dangerous story to tell. And here is a simple question that reveals the place of Mary: Who was the first person to tell this gospel story? No sooner did Gabriel return to God's presence than Mary dashed off to Elizabeth to tell her the story of Jesus. Mary was the first person to tell the gospel story about Jesus. Mary's gospel story about Jesus was eventually to become

Matthew and Mark and Luke and John, but if we could trace the earliest stories about Jesus to their first telling, we'd hear Mary's voice.

To tell the story of Jesus Mary needed, as all storytellers need, three things: some facts, a framework, and a narrative that pulls everything together. Mary accumulated facts faster than a D.C. journalist, and owing to the good graces of Gabriel, Mary had a framework for the gospel story. Jesus was to be understood as the Messiah, or as one of its rough equivalents—Son of God, Son of David, King, or Lord. And Mary had the Holy Spirit. Jesus would eventually tell his disciples, as told in the fourteenth and sixteenth chapters of John, that the Paraclete, the Holy Spirit, would "teach you all things and will remind you of everything I have said to you" and would "guide you into all the truth." Mary partook of that same Spirit as she began to tell others the story of Jesus.

Luke highlights something most of us skip over, and it is a clue that Mary first proclaimed the gospel about Jesus. After the shepherds revealed what the angels had said, Luke's Gospel tells us that "Mary treasured up all these things and pondered them in her heart."

What does it mean that Mary was treasuring and pondering? These are standard words in Judaism for thinking about events in one's life so one *could make sense of and narrate what God was doing in history*. To ponder is not to withdraw into silent meditation, as we might mean when we use the word "ponder," but *to deliberate in order to interpret*. Instead of imagining Mary sitting quietly meditating in some corner all alone, while everyone else was singing and dancing and clapping and dreaming of the end of Augustus' rule, Mary was actively figuring out what in the world God was doing in the world.

Mary pondered the tale of two kings: Augustus and Jesus. And she composed the story of Jesus in her head in order to proclaim it to others.

A story well told is powerful. Think of what fiction can do. The nineteenth century saw the abolishing of slavery not because the government decreed that it was against basic human rights, but because Harriet Beecher Stowe, in 1852, gathered up some raw facts and put them into a story called *Uncle Tom's Cabin*. By telling that story, she awakened the States to the problem. The twentieth century saw the end of apartheid in South Africa not solely by the exposure of the glaring facts of oppression, but because Alan Paton, in 1948, arranged some brutal facts into a narrative called *Cry the Beloved Country*. He turned apartheid in South Africa into a global issue in need of urgent resolution. The stories told by Harriet Beecher Stowe and by Alan Paton were dangerous stories.

The same applies to a story of a person's life, a biography—with its arranged facts, narrative framework, and narrative cohesion. Tell us the facts of a person's life, and we who read about them can analyze the details. Put those facts into storied form, a biography, and we will come to know the living reality of that person. Tell us a dangerous story, a story that threatens the unjust fabric of society, and you can change the world. That's what the Gospels are.

Without dismissing the important role played by the apostles or the Evangelists themselves, we must remember that the story now recorded in the Gospels began when Mary began to ponder and, after pondering, when Mary began to tell the story about Jesus to others. It is not that Mary sat down and wrote out a Gospel. There is no evidence of that. What Mary did was pass on the story orally—by word of mother.

What was the story she passed on? The gospel story Mary announced was the dangerous story that Jesus was King and Augustus was not. Mary's tale of two kings was dangerous the way Gutenberg's press and the radio and the television and the Internet are dangerous: She succeeded in getting the word out. Mary knew the facts, and she began to recount the story about Jesus that we now read in the Gospels.

The danger surrounding Mary and Jesus was about to take an even more serious turn. When it was all over, Mary would become a singular witness to all that God was doing in Israel through her son. Not only was the danger about to increase, but also Mary's story was about to get bigger.

5

"Where is the one who has been born king?"

What the real Mary witnessed began to add up. She heard from Gabriel, she heard from Joseph that he had heard from Gabriel, and she heard from Elizabeth who had heard from Zechariah who had heard from Gabriel who had heard from God. (Don't worry, the string doesn't get any longer than this.) She also heard from the shepherds who had heard from the angels who had heard from God.

What Mary witnessed added up to the promise that her son would establish the long-awaited Davidic dynasty. Gabriel, as we read in Luke's first chapter, declared that her son "will be great and will be called the Son of the Most High. The Lord God will give him the throne of his father David, and he will reign over the house of Jacob forever; his kingdom will never end." Those were same words that were used in the promise given to David back in the seventh chapter of Second Samuel.

These promises that Mary witnessed led her to think that God would soon set her son on David's throne in Jerusalem, defeat the Romans with their own swords, escort them to a Roman road in their own chariots, or send them back to Italy in their own boats.

These were her conclusions to the words she heard and the visions she witnessed. There would be more to come, not the least of which was the significance of holding a baby in her arms, the result of a miraculous conception.

Witness of a body
Jesus' birth was real in spite of what we hear in the sentimental Christmas song *Away in a Manger*. Notice these words:

Away in a manger,
no crib for his bed,
the little Lord Jesus laid down his sweet head.
The stars in the bright sky looked down where he lay,
The little Lord Jesus asleep on the hay.

The cattle are lowing, the baby awakes,
But little Lord Jesus no crying he makes.

This scene is tranquil, peaceful, idyllic, oozing with warm thoughts and gentle feelings—like a Thomas Kinkade painting.

All we need is a flush of amber and mauve and a toasty fireplace. The cattle are lowing and they awaken Jesus with his cute, sweet head. The song continues with "no crying he makes." But real newborns do cry—that's one of the rules.

I know that when Christmas comes this year, I'll probably toss my own voice into the mix when our church sings this carol again, but it has little to do with the realities of Jesus' birth.

Here's what most likely happened to Mary at Jesus' birth. While Joseph and Mary were in Bethlehem, the time for her delivery came and, because there was no room in the "inn," they found another place. The word translated *inn* in most of our Bibles does not refer to a hotel. Why? A small hamlet like Bethlehem wasn't large enough for a hotel. Most historians today think they were more likely guests in a home where there were two parts to the home: family quarters (upstairs), which is sometimes called an "inn," and animal quarters (downstairs) where the "manger" was.

Either because Mary preferred—out of a sense of decency or purity—more room for the privacy of a birth or because there were too many other guests in the "inn," she moved downstairs into the animal quarters for the birth. Moving into those quarters probably had nothing to do with unkind innkeepers or inhospitable homeowners, even if that makes for a good story.

The birth of Jesus was real. When Mary gave birth, she probably had a midwife, because in the Jewish world women gave medical care to women. In the absence of a midwife, Joseph would have performed the duties of a midwife. Mary probably delivered Jesus from a birthing stool with a back and grips, which was also shaped with a crescent-shaped bottom so the baby could slide through into the safe grasp of the midwife. Like all mothers, she was in pain. The midwife (or Joseph) would have then taken care of the baby and Mary as well as the blood and afterbirth. Mary then, Luke's Gospel tells us, wrapped the baby in "swaddling cloths" to keep Jesus warm and safe, and then she laid Jesus to rest "in a manger." Think of a shelf of stones with a slight depression or (less likely) a feeding trough constructed of wood. Such things are not designed for babies, especially one with a "sweet" head.

It matters that Jesus had a real body. For Jesus to be really human he had to be born, as the apostle Paul wrote in the fourth chapter of his letter to the Galatians, *of* a woman and not just *through* a woman. God didn't just use Mary as a "rent-a-womb" but actually became DNA—Mary's. The theological expression at work here is "incarnation," and the underlying principle is this: What God becomes, God redeems. God becomes what we are—with a real body—so we can become children of God. That's why Jesus' real body is important for our faith.

For Mary there was another issue. When Mary held that newborn little body in her hands, Mary witnessed the living reality of the promise Gabriel had made to her nine months earlier. She was holding the promise-come-true. The real body she held proved to her that what God said really would take place.

For theologians, the birth of Jesus is about the "incarnation." That is, that God became real human flesh. Yet, for Mary the birth of Jesus was about "coronation." I doubt Mary thought in the terms theologians use today. I doubt she wondered if her son was God *and* human or the God-man or what about his natures and person—how they were related. That's the stuff of theological discussion. For the real Mary, that live body named Jesus may have been a messy, fussy, physical little body, but that real body was an undeniable witness to the truth that God could work miracles. If God could bring a pregnancy from a miraculous conception to a real birth, then the promise that her son would be the Davidic king on the throne in Israel was also the next promise to be fulfilled.

And what happened next proved this to her.

Witness from the Magi

Matthew's second chapter informs us that some Gentile Magi from the East came to Mary's home and worshiped Jesus, giving him extravagant gifts. Originally, the word *Magi* referred to a priestly caste in Persia, but the term came to mean "magician" and "astrologer" as well. Magi were widely known and respected in the Gentile world for their capacity to interpret dreams. Because Magi were always censured in the Bible for dabbling in the mysteries that belong exclusively to God, their cosmically guided presence before Mary surprised her.

It is difficult to know what Mary thought. When they offered their gifts to her Messiah son, did she think their action was an indication that astrology and magic were coming to an end? Or, did she think that this was just one more extraordinary event in the list of things she had recently witnessed? Or, was her mind in tune with the many Old Testament passages where Gentiles would stream to Jerusalem to worship Israel's God when the kingdom arrived? Was she remembering Isaiah's eleventh chapter, where we read that when the Messiah came he would "stand as a banner for the peoples; the *nations* will rally to him"? Or Jeremiah's third chapter: "At that time they [Judah] will call Jerusalem The Throne of the LORD, and *all nations* will gather in Jerusalem to honor the name of the Lord"? How could she not also have thought that these were the foretold *Gentiles* of the Scriptures, who would offer gifts to Israel's future king?

A related fact deserves our consideration: Matthew's Gospel brings the Magi into personal contact with none other than Herod the Great, the one who was himself threatened by the arrival of Jesus the Messiah. The Magi, Matthew's second chapter tells us, went immediately into Jerusalem and asked, "Where is the one who has been born king of the Jews?" Herod summoned the biblical interpreters together to find out where the Messianic king would be born. They informed him that this king would be born in Bethlehem, and they quoted Micah's fifth chapter to prove their conclusion: "But you, Bethlehem . . . out of you will come for me a ruler over Israel." Because of the Magi's knowledge that a rival king was now alive in the Land of Israel, Herod the Great, not aware that the future king was in Bethlehem, "called the Magi secretly and found out from them the exact time the star had appeared." He then instructed the Magi to report back to him after their visit so that he, too, could worship the king. As we read the Gospel of Matthew's story about these and subsequent events, it is clear that Herod was lying—he wanted to know where Jesus was so he could kill him and end any rival to his dynasty.

Connecting the Magi with Herod brings into living reality what Mary declared in the Magnificat: Jesus is king, Herod the Great is not. When the Magi found their way to Herod the

Great, they didn't fall on their faces before him. Yet Mary witnessed the Magi offering her son gifts meant for a king, gifts Herod the king might have expected for himself. If you simply back up to what Mary had witnessed—angels declaring her son to be king, relatives doing the same, and shepherds making the same claim, you would arrive at Mary's conclusion: Jesus will be king and Herod the Great will not be.

The Gentile Magi "bowed down and worshiped" Jesus, and then, as we read in Matthew's second chapter, "they opened their treasures"—as one would do for a king. It must have been a strange sight: Gentiles to begin with, Magi on top of that, a suspicious encounter with Herod the Great and the ruling priests in Jerusalem, and then an unannounced visitation of these Magi at the home of Joseph and Mary.

But who were the real Magi? We are not sure how many Magi there were, we are not sure of their origin (Babylonia or Persia perhaps), we are not sure they were kings even though we were taught to sing *We Three Kings from Orient Are* at Christmastime, and we are not sure where they visited the holy family. We infer that there were three Magi because there were three gifts—"gifts of gold, frankincense and myrrh." Some early Christians gave them names and they have stuck—Gaspar, Melchior, and Balthasar. We are not even sure they visited the holy family in Bethlehem or two or more years later in Nazareth, though the text of Luke suggests they came to Bethlehem, and Matthew's account reads as if their visit happened immediately after the birth. But we really don't know.

What we do know is that Mary witnessed Gentile Magi arriving at her home with gifts for a king. How could she not have thought that this meant her son would have significance well beyond the borders of the Land of Israel? How could she not have also thought that her son might have significance all the way to the throne in Rome? Mary was too sharp not to have made these connections: When you witness such wonders things begin to add up.

There's plenty more to add before some subtraction begins.

Witness from a star

In the ancient world it was not uncommon for a report to circulate that a star appeared when a king was born. Tacitus, a first-century Roman historian, once said during the reign of Nero that the "general belief is that a comet means a change of emperor." Trailing the Magi into the home of Mary and Joseph was the story of a star that guided them from their foreign country to the very place where Jesus was.

How do we explain the star? Some suggest the star appeared as a supernova. Others suggest that a comet's appearance in about 12 or 11 BC should be connected to the Magi's star. Yet others, through the study of historical records, conjecture a planetary conjunction of Jupiter and Saturn and Mars. Johannes Kepler estimated that such a conjunction occurred in 7 or 6 BC. And yet others, who are more likely here to be on the side of the angels, think this is a miracle star.

Whether or not Mary saw the star, she would have been told about that star by the Gentile Magi. A little newborn body, some Gentiles, and now a star—all witnesses to her son. And this great cloud of witnesses was growing.

Witness from an angel

Everything added up to the word *danger*. Mary's baby was a threat to Herod the Great and to Caesar Augustus, and now people from all over the world knew thanks to the news from the Magi. Mary knew Herod would soon be on the prowl for her son Jesus. What would Mary do to protect her son?

That's why God created angels—like Gabriel.

When we first met Gabriel he was a conception-message angel: He told Zechariah that Elizabeth would conceive, Mary that she would conceive, and Joseph that Mary had conceived. He was also a birth-message angel: He told the shepherds that Jesus had been born. But Gabriel (we assume it is the same angel) was also a protection-message angel: He informed the Magi not to go back to Herod and to return home another way.

The angel then appeared to Joseph to inform him that, as Matthew's second chapter informs us, "Herod is going to search for the child to kill him." Therefore, Joseph was to "take the child and his mother and escape to Egypt." Joseph did as the angel told him. During their sojourn in Egypt, Herod—on the prowl for newborn kings—slaughtered the infants of Bethlehem—an act consistent with Herod's mania for power. After the good news that Herod had died (in 4 BC), the protection-message angel appeared again to Joseph in a dream and declared to him that he could return to Nazareth safely. And they made the long trek back.

Mary witnessed these angelic events.

By the time she and Joseph returned to dwell in Nazareth, we have to think that Mary was asking God, "Haven't we had enough?"

Mary as witness

At this point in her journey, Mary had pondered a story that marched rather boldly in one direction: Her son would rule from Jerusalem as the Davidic king, and he would establish the Davidic dynasty once and for all. From the first word out of Gabriel's mouth to the arrival of the Magi, everything added up in one direction: Jesus would become king and neither Herod the Great nor Caesar Augustus would be. Mary was a witness of these extraordinary promises about her son who would become king. And God's protecting the child from Herod, along with the family's brief sojourn in Egypt, also informed her how protected his kingship would be.

But what happened next would lead Mary to reshape the story of her son. In the next chapter and the chapters that follow we will discover a different Mary: a Mary who struggled, sometimes rather demandingly, with the details of her son's life and ministry. Her struggles, if we follow her in her real world, were also the struggles of every person around Jesus. In the simplest of terms, Jesus neither acted like the Messiah they expected nor taught what Mary and his disciples expected. Mary struggled with Jesus because he didn't conform to her all-too-common image of what the Messiah's life and rule would look like.

But that's getting ahead of our story.

For Mary, things were about to change. On Jesus' fortieth day of earthly existence, Luke's second chapter tells us that Joseph and Mary took Jesus to the Temple for a dual ceremony: Mary's purification and Jesus' dedication. At the Temple, they encountered an old man who challenged Mary to modify her story of Jesus. What was starting to be an exciting game of addition of witnesses was about to become a game of subtraction.

6

" A sword will pierce your own soul "
WOMAN OF SORROW

During the delivery of our firstborn, Laura, I fainted in the delivery room. While a kind nurse attended to me with a cup of coffee, Kris and the nurses worked to bring Laura into this world. (I'd have to guess about the details because I was flat on the floor.) After I came to my senses, I was escorted politely to a waiting area. Eventually they wheeled Kris back to her room, and then took me to the room where we both got to hold Laura and talk about how beautiful she was (and still is). It was already early into the next morning, so I drove home and left Kris to begin recovering. I came back the next day and sat around, and we talked about how beautiful Laura was, and then again I went home. The next day, if my memory serves me right, we brought Laura home to some fanfare: The whole family was there to help. The women all seemed to know what to do; I sure didn't. So, like a good dad, I watched a basketball game. It was nearly the same with our son Lukas three years later, except I didn't faint and we watched a different game. We didn't do anything official; we just welcomed our new children into our family.

At our church, we didn't have anything official for either of our kids. We were in a church at the time that not only didn't baptize infants, it didn't even go in for baptism's non-sacramental substitute, the Baby Dedication service, where pastors pray over crying babies watched by admiring parents and grandparents and family members. We all simply began bringing our new ones to church.

Not so in the Jewish world of Mary, Joseph, and Jesus. Jewish families had several official religious ceremonies after the birth of the firstborn. Three distinct ceremonies were intertwined: the circumcision of the son (at which time he was named), the consecration of the firstborn, and the purification of the mother. Here is what the twelfth chapter of Leviticus said about the circumcision and the mother's purification:

> The LORD said to Moses, "Say to the Israelites: a woman who becomes pregnant and gives birth to a son will be ceremonially unclean for seven days, just as she is unclean during her monthly period. On the eighth day the boy is to be circumcised. Then the woman must wait thirty-three days to be purified from her bleeding. She must not touch anything sacred or go to the sanctuary until the days of her purification are over."

Luke chapter two tells us that on the eighth day, Mary and Joseph did what the Torah prescribed: They circumcised their son and named him "Jesus." Forty days or more after the birth the Torah required them to go to Jerusalem to the Temple so Jesus could be consecrated and Mary purified. "Consecrate to me," the LORD tells Moses, in Exodus 13, "every firstborn male. The first offspring of every womb among the Israelites belongs to me, whether human or animal."

For Mary's purification, Joseph purchased two turtledoves. Soon they would offer them in the Temple to restore Mary to full participation in Temple worship and social relations. It is noticeable that Joseph and Mary purchased two turtle-doves. The Law specified a lamb but, if the family was too poor to offer a lamb, two turtledoves substituted instead of a lamb. "One of the riddles," the American New Testament scholar Catherine Clark Kroeger observes, "with which Mary must wrestle is that of the exalted promises concerning her child and the impoverished circumstances attendant to the birth." The irony that the mother of the future king was offering a poor person's sacrifice would have been palpable to Mary.

On their way into the Temple to dedicate Jesus and purify Mary lightning struck.

Glory before the sorrow

No sooner did Mary cross the threshold of the Temple than an old man, named Simeon, swept the baby from their arms and cried out a song of relief, of declaration, and of prophecy. (Eventually Joseph and Mary will also name one of their boys "Simeon." Were they thinking of this Simeon or of the head of one of the twelve tribes of Israel or both?)

Simeon's words as found in Luke's second chapter are often called the *Nunc Dimittis,* after the first two words in the Latin translation. His words immediately confirm what Joseph and Mary already believed about Jesus: that he would become Israel's king. (Read his words slowly.)

Sovereign Lord, as you have promised,
>> you may now dismiss [nunc dimittis] your servant in peace.
>>> For my eyes have seen your salvation,
>>>> which you have prepared in the sight of all nations:
>>> a light for revelation to the Gentiles,
>>> and the glory of your people Israel.

Simeon boldly announced that Mary's son would bring not only comfort to Israel but also redemption and peace to the whole world. Like a good orator, Simeon began with the glory before he turned to the sorrow.

Way of sorrow

What Simeon said next began the slow, methodical process of subtracting elements of Mary's vision of the Messiah's kingdom: the Davidic dynasty would be less than, and different from, what she expected.

I consider the next words to be a turning point in Mary's life. Up to this point, Mary's view of the kingdom was traditional and triumphal. But in using the simple image of a sword, Simeon revealed that the traditional and triumphal theory of a Davidic dynasty was not the whole story. Simeon's words revealed that the Davidic triumph would come, not through military victory, but through death on a cross. Let's look at theses words a little more closely.

Simeon's words opened up a foreboding future to Joseph and Mary: *"This child is destined to cause the falling and rising of many in Israel, and to be a sign that will be spoken against, so that the thoughts of many hearts will be revealed. And a sword will pierce your own soul too."* Simeon announced that the future king's glory would come through sorrow and suffering. With the image of the sword, Simeon announced the cross, and that cross subtracted from Mary's vision her idea of the crown and tore in half the fabric of the very story Mary was weaving.

We cannot be fair to the real Mary until we learn to observe her life as it unfolded. It is easy to think of Mary in simple, pious terms—of a Mary who knew her son was the Son of God, or of a Mary for whom every prophecy and event that happened made sense to her as it happened. But that is not the real Mary, and it is not the Mary we discover in the Gospels themselves.

What Mary heard from Simeon stunned her. Everything she had so far heard from angels and Joseph and relatives and shepherds and the Gentile magi suggested a victorious kind of Messiah, the sort of Messiah everyone embraced as God's hope for Israel. Mary's son would be king of Israel, Simeon predicted. Yet, this king-son of hers would also be rejected and maligned and made a center of controversy. Mary was the mother of the Messiah. Yes, but a "sword" would pierce her soul. "A sword?" she must have asked. Historians have wracked their brains and shaken the last possible piece of fruit from every tree in the Bible in order to come to terms with what Simeon meant when he spoke of a "sword."

The simplest way to explain what Simeon said to Mary is to go directly to the words of Jesus in the tenth chapter of

Matthew, because his words use the metaphor of a sword: "Do not suppose that I have come to bring *peace* to the earth. *I did not come to bring peace, but a sword.* For I have come to turn a man against his father, a daughter against her mother, a daughter-in-law against her mother-in-law—your enemies will be the members of your own household." (It is worth pondering whether Jesus may have first heard this sword metaphor when his mother told him what Simeon had said to his parents in the Temple. Was it possible for Mary *not* to have told Jesus what Simeon had said in the Temple?)

What Simeon meant by this "sword" can be reduced to four simple sentences:

Jesus will be king.
As king he will judge the nation.
But Jesus will be rejected.
Mary will suffer, too.

Simeon's words meant that the much-anticipated overthrow of Herod the Great and the routing of Caesar Augustus would come at great cost—to her son and to herself. Her son was born to be king, but the crown her son was to wear would be a cross. The story Mary was learning to tell about Jesus had to change.

Let me ask a question that can help us consider what it was like for Mary to hear Simeon's words: How would it strike you if, when leaving the hospital after a birth or when leaving the church after your child's baptism or dedication, some aged stranger grabbed your infant into his arms and, with a smile on his face, began extolling the greatness of your child? (Would you feel wondrous and proud and honored?) And, what if for months ahead of your delivery angels and relatives had told you that your child would be the next ruler of the world? (Would you find this old man's words just what the doctor ordered?) What if then, with a sudden change in countenance, the old man looked you in the eye and declared that your child would be despised and rejected and that your child would be a source of much sorrow for you? (Would you be bewildered and numbed? Would you begin to ponder and brood?) That, and more, was Mary's experience that day in the Temple courts.

The return and sorrow

When the brief time with Simeon ended, Mary and Joseph left the Temple to return home. That original trip from Bethlehem was full of excitement; the trip back to Nazareth combined the joy of pondering a baby born-to-be-king with the brooding silence of pondering a king-to-be-crucified. Is that what Mary had dedicated her son to be when she and Joseph went to the Temple? Mary meditated on what she had learned about Jesus. She had gone to the Temple as the Torah required, but she left the Temple thinking much less about Torah require-ments and far more about the one who was predicted by the prophets. What did they say about the Messiah? Did they predict the sword of Simeon? She would learn the answers by observing her son.

The flash of the sword predicted by Simeon was the beginning of sorrow for Mary. As we accompany Mary in her journey with Jesus we will see how difficult it was, not only for her but for everyone else who loved and followed him, to put together the strange story Jesus' life would tell. Messiahs and crosses didn't mesh in the Jewish theology Mary knew. The framework of her faith and tradition conflicted with what she learned that day from Simeon and from what she would see in the life of Jesus.

Twelve years later, in that very Temple area where Simeon spoke of that mysterious sword, Jesus would give Mary and Joseph one more indication that Jesus' life would not turn out as they expected. The Son of God, they would learn, listened to the heart of a different Father (and mother). Mary would then learn to follow her son.

7
"In my Father's house"
WOMAN OF WONDER

In the United States we celebrate America's independence on the Fourth of July. Most Americans probably do not spend the day thinking about England's King George III and the Boston Tea Party of 1773, nor do we think much about the separation of church and state. Most think about family and picnics and what to barbecue. Kris and I usually take the short walk down the street to our high school baseball field where, with hundreds of others, we find a good spot for our lawn chairs so we can watch the fireworks.

I do not begin my day thinking about the Declaration of Independence of 1776 or the meaning of freedom. In fact, if I am honest, the Fourth of July has little to do with the word "independence" or "liberation" in my life. It is mostly a family holiday. Why? I take our freedom for granted. I don't say this lightly, but honestly.

But imagine this with me: If—and this begins a series of big hypothetical "ifs"—the already free United States were captured by a foreign country, and if we were forced to act as some foreign ruler wanted us to, *and if that government permitted us to celebrate the Day of Independence,* I suspect our perception of July Fourth would change. We might all gather together to read publicly *The Declaration of Independence,* and we might all pray to God to grant us our freedom again. Instead of taking freedom for granted, we'd be longing for freedom.

That is what Passover was like for Joseph, Mary, and Jesus. Rome occupied the Land and a Gentile governor—named Coponius—ruled, but nonetheless Rome permitted Israel to celebrate the Jewish equivalent of our Day of Independence, *Passover,* a holiday designed to evoke memories of liberation. Israel gathered into families, and the father of the household read the Passover story. The celebration encouraged Israel to dream big dreams about independence and liberation and no parents in Israel had deeper dreams about liberation than the parents of Jesus. On the last day of one such Passover celebration, Jesus revealed something about himself that made Mary wonder who her son really was and what kind of liberation he would bring.

Wondering at Passover

Passover brewed a savory pot of family fellowship, renewed social friendships with fellow Jews throughout the Land, and evoked sacred memories of liberation from slavery. Joseph and Mary faithfully observed Passover, for Luke tells us that they went "every year" to Jerusalem for the celebration. Each year they renewed fellowship with Mary's relative Elizabeth and her husband Zechariah (as long as they were alive), and Jesus spent time with his relatives such as John, the future Baptist, as well as with his cousins James and John, the future apostles. They probably explored Jerusalem with one another, so by the time Jesus came to Jerusalem for that last supper, he and the others knew Jerusalem intimately.

Passover's central theme was politically sensitive: *liberation*. Passover celebrations, now known to us through the Jewish Passover *Seder*, physically re-enacted the liberation of the children of Israel from Egyptian slavery at the hand of the world's most powerful ruler at the time, Pharaoh. This theme ignited the suspicions and fears of Rome's puppet kings in Israel while it also inflamed the hopes of those Jews who suffered under Roman policies. Passover provoked Israelites to *wonder* about liberation, to ponder Israel's past freedom, and to dream of Israel's future freedom.

For Mary especially, Passover would have been an opportunity to wonder about the promised liberation her son would bring. Everything she had witnessed indicated her son would bring that liberation—and no event in Israel's history evoked that liberation like Passover. Joseph and Mary must have winked at one another when they heard other Israelites long for liberation or even when they heard speculation about who would be the next ruler of Israel. They must have wondered what their son's kingdom would be like, and Mary soon began to wonder what kind of son Jesus would be.

Wondering about her missing son

Luke's second chapter tells us that Jesus was *twelve* when he attended one such Passover with Joseph and Mary: "Every year Jesus' parents went to Jerusalem for the Festival of the Passover. When he was twelve years old, they went up to the Festival, according to the custom." Why does Luke tell us Jesus was "twelve"? Was this perhaps Luke's way of saying this was Jesus' personal *bar mitzvah*, the day Jesus became a "son of the Torah," the day Jesus was liberated from his parents to become an adult? From what we know from historical records, the *bar mitzvah* ceremony did not officially develop until several hundred years after Jesus' life. Yet, whether or not this was Jesus' official *bar mitzvah* experience, at this Passover Jesus clearly went public as an adult male, liberating himself for the moment from his parents and family, and his behavior made everyone wonder what kind of person Jesus was.

We might do some wondering ourselves. When I think of twelve-year-old boys today and I compare them to Jesus in the Temple at twelve, "I scarce can take it in"—to use those famous words from *How Great Thou Art*. Twelve-year-olds, as I know them, worry about what that they look like in order that they might both look like one another and unlike their parents and teachers. They worry about whether they should wear sandals or Nikes when they go to the mall, whether their jeans are designer, whether others will see their pimples, and whether they have a cool enough cell phone. Boys are still playing Little League baseball and riding bicycles, and their voices are just beginning to descend. I've coached twelve-year-old boys, and the best thing about them is that they don't remain twelve-year-olds forever.

When Jesus was twelve, Joseph and Mary and their extended family had caravanned from Nazareth up to Jerusalem for Passover. Caravans sometimes involved as many as a hundred or more "family" members. When the caravan headed back to Nazareth after the week-long Passover celebrations, Jesus remained at the Temple. The traveling group was large enough and freedom for the young boys wide enough that Mary and Joseph did not notice Jesus' absence until the end of the first day's trip. When they discovered their son as missing, and Mary would have experienced his absence as only the mother of a missing child can, the caravan was already about twenty miles north of Jerusalem. Wondering about their missing son, Mary and Joseph first checked with their companions and, not finding Jesus, they began the arduous task of returning to Jerusalem. This cost them another day's trip. Then Luke tells us that it took them yet another day of scouring Jerusalem and its environs before they found him sitting among teachers in the Temple courts, asking questions and providing answers.

Observe that in the Gospel of Luke the scene shifts at this point to Mary. Abruptly Mary (not Joseph) blurted out "Son," as the Gospel of Luke tells us at the end of chapter two, "Why have you treated us like this? Your father and I have been anxiously searching for you." Many of us know what it is like to be at a zoo or a big park or at a Cubs game when we lose sight of one of our children. Our heart is shocked with sudden terror until we can find our child again. The terror may only last a moment, but its reality burns deep into the heart of fear. Sometimes we have harsh words for our kids.

How do you think Mary felt after a day trip north and a long return trip to Jerusalem and then an entire day scouring Jerusalem in search of Jesus? Mary claimed that they had been "anxiously" searching for Jesus, and by using that term Mary expressed a heated, terrifying swelling of fear on her part that they had lost their messianic son. We all sympathize with Mary for being worried, and we will probably also sympathize with her if she was a bit shocked when she heard how Jesus responded to her question. What Jesus said made her wonder about who he was and what kind of liberation Jesus had in mind.

Wondering about her son's "Father"

"Why were you searching for me?" Luke tells us he asked. "Didn't you know I had to be in my Father's house?" Jesus' two questions expressed his surprise at his mother's worry and words. It is not hard to imagine what Mary thought when she heard those words. What would you say to your son who had been lost but whom you had just found after three frantic days of searching and muttering under your breath? What would you say if your son, in response, asked the questions Jesus asked? I know what I'd say, and I'm pretty sure I know what my wife would say. (You fill in the blanks.) That's just what Mary wanted to say, but there was something potent about what Jesus said, something surprising, and something that would make Mary wonder.

Jesus' second question was "Didn't you know I had to be *in my Father's house?*" "In my Father's house?" What did that expression mean to the real Mary who knew Jesus was not speaking about Joseph? In this question, Jesus revealed who he was: Jesus told Mary that God, the One God of Israel, was uniquely his Father.

And his relationship to *this* Father was unlike any relationship he had on earth. Jesus, at twelve, made it clear that his relationship to his mother was subordinate to his relationship to his Father.

When Mary heard these words of Jesus, she caught a momentary glimpse of the new relationship she would have with her son—and that glimpse made Mary wonder.

We need to back up to what Mary saw when she got to the Temple. Jesus, Luke's Gospel tells us, was *sitting* in the Temple courts surrounded by the Jewish teachers. The posture of "sitting" in the Jewish world of Temple teachers describes either a student *listening* to his rabbi or a rabbi *teaching* students around him. Luke tells us that Jesus was sitting, listening, asking, and answering. Most important, Jesus was at the center of a group of biblical scholars and theological experts. "Everyone," the Gospel of Luke tells us, "who *heard* him was amazed at his understanding and his answers." The words "heard" and "answers" reveals what was going on, and Mary witnessed this. The posture of Jesus was not that of a student *listening;* instead, he had assumed the posture of *teaching*—the leaders were *listening to Jesus* when he was twelve.

As Mary wondered about that very incident—and it might have taken her time to grasp this—she would naturally have connected Jesus to predictions in the Old Testament, perhaps even those about the Messiah in Isaiah chapter eleven, a text that Jews regularly recalled when they thought of the kingdom and the Messiah:

A shoot will come up from the stump of Jesse; from his roots a Branch will bear fruit.

The Spirit of the LORD will rest on him—
> the Spirit of *wisdom and of understanding*,
> the Spirit of counsel and of might,
> the Spirit of the knowledge and fear of the LORD—
> and he will delight in the fear of the LORD.

What Jesus was doing in the Temple evoked a common Jewish expectation: The messianic king, when he came to liberate Israel from its enemies, would be filled with God's Spirit and wisdom. What Mary saw that day when she found Jesus sitting in the Temple, however long it took her to grasp it, was that her son was the messianic king of wisdom. Notice that he was surrounded by a circle of listeners—and this anticipates a theme that will shape the next phase of Mary's life when she, as his mother, will learn to become a disciple of her son.

In the same location where Simeon had made his prediction of the Messiah's destiny to suffer, Jesus boldly announced his *vocation*: He had been dedicated to the Father in this Temple, and at twelve he revealed that his mission was to serve that Father. When Jesus said he had to be "in his Father's *house*," Jesus declared that he was the Son of the Father and that those who followed him could become members of his Father's house. The liberation Jesus would bring—and the next few chapters will show this—would begin not with a sword but with a circle of followers, a circle that would widen into the Church. Liberation would begin when small groups gathered together to make freedom a reality.

The story Mary had composed in her mind about who Jesus was and how his messianic life would be was shifting. It was at this moment, when Jesus was twelve, that Mary began to wonder if she really knew who this son of hers was. Mary had heard Gabriel's words about Jesus, and she had heard Elizabeth's words as well. Mary had participated in the prophetic insights that she expressed in the Magnificat, she had heard what the shepherds and the Magi had said, and she had heard the words of Simeon about the sword that would pierce her soul. Until that moment, everything had gone in the direction of a triumphal overthrow of Herod the Great's descendant, Herod Antipas, and Caesar Augustus—except those final dark words of Simeon. Now Simeon's words revealed a naked reality: Jesus declared that his mission held more importance than his relationship to his mother and father. Was this the sword Simeon had said would pierce her own heart?

What Mary glimpsed in the Temple that day plays out over the next two chapters of this book. Mary's sense of the kingdom as a Davidic dynasty would have to give way to the kingdom as a new kind of family, and the center of that new family would not be Joseph and Mary, but Jesus, the Lord, the Son of the Father.

8

"Do whatever he tells you"

WOMAN OF SURRENDER

The first of the Ten Commandments in the book of Exodus reads, "You shall have no other gods before me." The Fifth Commandment reads, "Honor your father and your mother so that you may live long in the Land the LORD your God is giving you." Yet, sometimes honoring God and honoring parents come into conflict with one another. At least once a semester I have this sort of dialogue with a student—Student: "I want to major in Biblical and Theological Studies (BTS)." I always ask this question first: "Which major do your parents think you should choose?" Student: "Something like business. My parents think a BTS Major is unemployable." After suggesting that a BTS Major is not as unemployable as some think, I then ask, "What do you want to major in?" Student: "BTS."

I then ask why. The student almost invariably responds, "Because I think God wants me to." Then the student asks me this question: "What do you think I should do?" And my standard response is, "I think you should do what God wants you to do. But I also think you should work this out with your parents." I say this because I believe we should do what God wants us to do in a way that honors our parents, so we can cling to both the First and the Fifth Commandments. Yet, sometimes doing what God wants brings us into conflict with what parents may want.

What did it mean to "honor" one's parents according to that Fifth Commandment? What would honoring one's parents mean to Jesus and Mary and Joseph? Honor, in the Judaism of the time, was the claim that parents (Joseph and Mary) had on their child (Jesus) to *display respect for them* in private and public places. As parents love and care for children, so children are to honor them for that love and care. In particular, as sons—including Jesus—matured, they were expected to secure their freedom from their parents in a way that neither humiliated nor impoverished their parents. As parents like Joseph and Mary aged, Israelite sons and daughters were to honor their parents by providing for them. The Jewish world, if we seek for analogies today, looked more like *Leave it to Beaver* or *The Waltons* than like *The Simpsons*.

We live in a different world. Western culture is a *rights* world. Instead of focusing on honor, American society consists of laws designed to protect each person's *rights*. Instead of focusing on rights as we do in our culture, ancient Jewish society focused on *duty*. The operative question everyone asked at all times was, "How *ought* I to behave in light of my status in society?" Rather than the questions asked in our society—"What do *I* want to do?" or "What are my rights?"—Mary's Jewish society asked, "What *should* I do?" or "What does *my culture expect* me to do?" Put directly, if Jesus coordinated his behavior with the cultural code, he brought honor to God, to Mary, to his family, to his society, and to himself—in precisely that order. In the ancient Jewish world, if Jesus instead chose not to coordinate his behavior with the cultural code, he dishonored Mary, his family, his society, and himself.

The Fifth Commandment to honor one's parents shaped nearly everything about Jewish society, but sometimes it came into conflict with the First Commandment to have no other gods before the Lord. When he was twelve, Jesus seemingly challenged this honor code; he remained in the Temple and then informed his parents that it was more important for him to be in *his Father's* house than to return to Nazareth with them. Jesus was saying that the First Commandment—"you shall have no other gods before me"—took precedence over the Fifth Commandment—"honor your father and your mother." Such a ranking of priorities can easily get out of hand, so it is important to observe that Jesus quickly showed his respect for the Fifth Commandment to honor his parents. At the end of Luke's second chapter we are informed that Jesus "went down to Nazareth with them and was obedient to them."

When Jesus challenged the limits of the honor-your-parents command some twenty years later at the wedding at Cana, the event began a public turning point in Mary's life. Mary, the mother, would learn to be obedient to her son. What she would have to learn, what she would have to struggle with in the real world—was that Jesus was in fact the one before whom she was to have no other gods. Mary would discover that obeying the First Commandment, honoring God above everything else, meant surrendering her own honor by following her own son!

At a wedding in Cana the real Mary learned this kind of obedience.

Challenging honor

Jesus, his mother, and his disciples had been invited to a wedding at Cana, which, like Nazareth, was considered backwater in comparison to big-city Jerusalem. They made the eight-mile trip from Nazareth north to this small village of Cana for the wedding celebration. The names of the wedding party are not mentioned in the second chapter of John, but most think it was the wedding of a close friend or even a relative of Mary.

Weddings in Judaism were mega-events and were laced up tightly with honor codes. After an approximately one-year betrothal, the bridegroom and his friends marched across town in the evening to the bride's home, where they gave speeches. The focal point was the pledge to be a good and honorable husband. After the speeches, everyone formed an honor-drenched public parade with a display of candle lights and local fanfare and music and dancing. The party traveled to the groom's father's home for the banquet and wedding ceremony. Depending on a person's financial condition, wedding celebrations could last up to a week.

At the wedding in Cana something happened that put the wedding family's honor at risk. According to later rabbinic records, the groom was under the honor code to provide plenty of food and drink for his guests. Mary detected that they had run out of wine. Why Mary was concerned is not clear, but perhaps she was concerned about this because she was family or perhaps because she was catering the wedding banquet or perhaps because it put her own honor at risk. For whatever reason, Mary decided to approach Jesus about the draining of supplies and said to him, "They have no more wine."

However we explain the end of the wine supply, Mary's observation that the wine was gone was filled with expectation that Jesus *should* fix the problem. We don't know what Mary expected—did she expect Jesus to perform a miracle? Did she expect him to inform the guests so they might not get unruly? We don't know. Details aside, it is clear that Jesus understood his mother's words as carrying an honor code, fifth-commandment-claim-as-a-mother on him to do something about the wine.

Mary expected Jesus to honor her and her request, but Jesus was about to put the Fifth Commandment to honor one's mother in its proper place. Here's what Jesus said to his mother's seemingly reasonable request: "Woman, why do you involve me?" Jesus' terse response, found in John's second chapter, surprises us. Did those words shame his mother? To begin with, the word *woman* seems harsh to us, but the Greek word here could also be translated or at least understood as a synonym for *mother*. In the Jewish world of Jesus, the terms woman and mother could be interchangeable. We see a perfect example of their interchangeability in the nineteenth chapter of John's Gospel. When Jesus turned to his mother at the cross to provide for her after he died, Jesus said to his mother, "*Woman*, here is your son."

Immediately Jesus then turned to John and said, "Here is your *mother.*" In the space of two sentences the word "mother" and "woman" are used synonymously. For Jesus to have used the word *woman* for his mother at the wedding in Cana was neither impolite nor rude.

The question Jesus asked of his mother at the wedding after he used the word *woman*—"Why do you involve me?"—made it clear to Mary that she had *intruded* into his space and into God's plan for his life. In short, Mary was meddling, the sort of thing a mother might do with her new daughter-in-law. Jesus' words were, in the words of a scholar of Greek grammar, "a polite request to refrain from interference and to leave the whole matter to him."

From Mary's point of view, her honor was at stake, but there was another kind of honor at work here that Mary would embrace. Jesus, as he made clear in the Temple when he was twelve and as he made abundantly clear throughout John's Gospel, listened to the Father as only the Son could. Because he listened as no one else could, what he did best brought honor to God. Notice these words from the heart of John's fifth chapter. To begin with, the Son does only what the Father does:

> Very truly I tell you, the Son can do nothing by himself; he can do only what he sees his Father doing, because whatever the Father does the Son also does.

In fact, the Father shows the Son how to do everything.

> For the Father loves the Son and shows him all he does. Yes, and he will show him even greater works than these, so that you will be amazed. For just as the Father raises

the dead and gives them life, even so the Son gives life to whom he is pleased to give it. Moreover, the Father judges no one, but has entrusted all judgment to the Son, . . .

Therefore, Jesus says, to honor the Father one must honor the Son! He continues:

. . . that all may honor the Son just as they honor the Father. Whoever does not honor the Son does not honor the Father, who sent him.

For Jesus, honoring his Father was Commandment Number One. But, because Jesus was the Son of that Father and because whatever Jesus did was what the Father sent him to do, honoring the Son was how one honored the Father.

Mary's expectation for Jesus to get up and do something about the wine somehow conflicted with what Jesus understood to be the Father's expectations for him. We cannot now be sure how Mary could have known this, but that is not the point: Jesus challenged Mary to honor God the Father by honoring the Son, and by honoring God she had to let Jesus do *what* his Father sent him to do *when* the Father wanted it done.

Surrendering honor to her son

"My hour has not yet come," Jesus said to his mother. These words in John's Gospel are profoundly important for understanding a new development in Mary's relationship with Jesus. The little word "hour" is one of the apostle John's special words. Readers today sometimes miss this: In the Gospel of John, the *hour* is the time when Jesus will be glorified *by being crucified*. Not only this: Jesus was claiming to be the only one in the Land of Israel who knew when that hour would occur. Mary stood there and listened to her son make the incredible claim that he alone knew the Father's will and the Father's timing.

Now observe this, and see what Mary would have understood: If Jesus alone knew God's will, then the only ones who knew God's will were the ones to whom *Jesus* revealed that will. For Mary to know and do God's will, she would have to follow Jesus. Her honor would have to surrender to his honor. Jesus' words were subtle, and they pierced Mary's heart. She would have to allow her son to become her Lord.

This interchange between Mary and Jesus is nothing short of stunning.

If we draw together these details from this wedding, we see that Jesus was summoning his mother to surrender to him and to learn just as his disciples had learned when he commanded them: "Follow me!" Honor of parents, in Jesus' case, was turned upside down: Mary could receive honor only when she honored her own son.

Did Mary respond appropriately to Jesus' summons to honor God by following him? Evidently. Notice her next words. As instantaneously as responding "Yes, sir!" to a wise superior, Mary directs the servants at the wedding to "do whatever he tells you." Yes, Mary learned. We see this by observing how she responded to the words of Jesus at the wedding in Cana. She realized that when Jesus said, "My hour has not yet come," he was making a powerful claim to know God's will, and that anyone who wanted to bring honor to God would have to listen to Jesus, her son.

The glory of surrender

Mary's response turned the key that unlocked the door to Jesus' first miracle. Let us not minimize Mary's role in this first miracle, as we Protestants are prone to do. Because Mary directed the servants to do as Jesus said and because the servants obeyed, Jesus converted six thirty-gallon jars of water into the best wine yet served at that wedding. The groom and his family were spared a public shaming, and Jesus "revealed his glory"—as John's second chapter tells us. 180 gallons of wine was a profuse amount. That's about 700 bottles of wine, and that would mean that the family would be drinking wedding wine longer than most families today today eat wedding cake after a wedding.

John's Gospel calls this water-into-abundant-wine miracle a "sign." What is a sign? Is it just another word for "miracle"? Hardly. The Gospel of John uses the term *sign* when a simple miracle (Jesus did something stupendous like turning water into wine) is simultaneously a bottomless revelation of God's glory (Jesus revealed the glory of God's truth in that miracle). To call a miracle a *sign* is to claim that this miracle can be contemplated and pondered and turned around and over, and the more you contemplate and ponder that miracle, the deeper it leads us into the very heart of who Jesus is for us.

The "sign" of the water-into-wine, like the little origami figures that children learn to make in school, unfolds into all kinds of sizes and shapes. The wine miracle, when unfolded by contemplating the biblical images, speaks of joy, it speaks of the final banquet, and it speaks of new life. In addition, this profuse, abundant wine speaks of the transformation of Jewish purity jars into Jesus' wine of joy and of the old covenant being transformed into the new covenant. But mostly this water-become-wine reveals something about Jesus: that he makes all things abundantly and joyfully new and brimming with life. In fact, the sign here tells us that Jesus is himself the one who provides joy for those who will taste him and his provisions, who listen to his words, believe his words, and receive his words as words from the Father. The claim of the sign at Cana is that Jesus' life, brimming as it is with God's living presence, will never run dry and will always sustain his followers.

There are many spiritual riches here to contemplate, and it is doubtful that Mary or anyone at the wedding grasped the potency of the sign when it occurred. But, all of this was there—in rudimentary and elementary form—so that the eyes of faith could be opened to see who Jesus was.

That sign was triggered when Mary said, "Do whatever he tells you." We often forget her role here. Jesus did not perform the miracle-become-sign, the water-become-wine, until Mary directed the servants to do whatever Jesus said. Mary meddled in Jesus' business, Jesus revealed to her that he did only what the Father told him to do and only when the Father wanted it done, and Mary trusted those words of her son. By trusting Jesus, Mary unlocked the doors to a mighty miracle. But, Mary first had to surrender her own honor to her son. The Gospel of John suggests Mary stumbled into this, the way many of us stumble into faith.

Ongoing surrender

No one, including Mary, had Jesus all figured out. The Bible shows that God was revealing his plan slowly throughout Jesus' life, and there was plenty left to divulge. As God revealed ever-new things about Jesus, each follower would have to respond personally to those revelations—that he was Messiah, that he was rejected, and that he was crucified (yet rose again). The stories suggest that responding even to the miracles of Jesus was difficult for all of them. In fact, John's sixth chapter tells us that some of those who had been following Jesus decided to abandon him. No, they didn't have Jesus' signs and teachings figured out. For each of his followers, including Mary, it would take time to comprehend what was the Messiah's mission.

The apostle Peter, for example, may have seen very early something of the Jewish Messiah in this Jesus of Nazareth, and later he may have confessed his sin and followed Jesus with more enthusiasm than the others, but that did not prevent Peter from being utterly astounded when Jesus divulged that—in his role as Messiah—he would die at the hands of the Jewish leaders. Mary, too, faced the same struggle with who Jesus was. What she learned from her son that day at the wedding was that the First Commandment, to honor and worship God, was obeyed by following her son, the Son of the Father.

When Jesus was twelve, he distanced himself from Mary and Joseph because he had to be about his Father's business in his Father's house. At the wedding in Cana, Jesus again distanced himself from Mary by revealing that he alone, as the Son, knew the Father's will and knew when to bring it about. These two incidents of distancing himself from his mother both brought flesh to Simeon's warning about the sword that would pierce Mary's heart and revealed to Mary that only those who followed Jesus were part of the family of the Father of Jesus. Mary did not embrace these revelations swiftly. Like everyone else, she had to learn that her son was her Lord, and the family he was creating would become her family, too.

9

"Who are my mother and my brothers?"
WOMAN OF AMBIVALENCE

For Mary and for Jesus' siblings to relate to Jesus as the Messiah would have been difficult. But, for them to have confessed Jesus as Lord would have been unfathomable. If we think of Jesus' mother and the rest of the family gathering around Jesus daily "for church" in order to listen to him tell some parabolic sermons, we are making a big mistake. The real Mary and the real siblings and the real relatives of Jesus were ambivalent about Jesus—perhaps much of the time.

Their biggest problem was their Bible! It may surprise you, but Jesus' family had learned to read the prophetic portions in the Old Testament in a specific way for signs of the foretold Messiah. That reading created their ambivalence about him. To prevent us from getting impatient with Mary, we need to slow down long enough to understand what Jewish teaching suggested the Messiah would be like.

The typical Jewish understanding of the Messiah combined at least four Old Testament figures into one, and we will do well to take a brief look at each.

First, Jews expected the Messiah to be, as Deuteronomy 18 predicted, a "prophet like *Moses*."

Second, Jews expected the Messiah to be like, but transcend Israel's *prophets* of old. Thus, as we read in the sixteenth chapter of Matthew, when Jesus asks his disciples who they think he is, it is only after they ponder whether or not Jesus is a prophetic figure—"others say Elijah; and still others, Jeremiah or one of the prophets"—that Peter can finally pull all those images together into one word: "You are the *Messiah*."

Third, everyone associated the Messiah with *David*, for the Messiah would be a descendant of David. If God promised, as he did in 2 Samuel 7, that there would always be a Davidic king on the throne, then the final Messiah would have to be a Davidic king.

And, fourth, when the Messiah reigned, he would combine the glory of David with the wisdom of *Solomon*. Why? Solomon's storied life emerged from his brilliant decision to ask God for wisdom, as 1 Kings 3 tells us: "So give your servant a discerning heart to govern your people and to distinguish between right and wrong." Later Solomon redirected that gift of wisdom onto paper when he wrote the book of Proverbs. Then Isaiah 11, looking like a paragraph drawn from the wisdom of Proverbs' first chapter, predicts a Solomon-like figure as the future messianic king: "The Spirit of the Lord will rest on him—the Spirit of wisdom and of understanding, the Spirit of counsel and of might, the Spirit of the knowledge and fear of the Lord."

Thus, when we put all of this together, the future Messiah would be like Moses, mentoring everyone to obey the Torah; like a prophet, declaring the word of the Lord in thunderous and poetic terms; like David the king, sitting on the throne in peace after conquering the Land and routing the enemies of Israel; and like Solomon, offering wisdom to the people. The Messiah would be each of these, and more. As Jesus said at the end of Matthew's twelfth chapter, "and now one greater than Solomon is here."

The Psalms of Solomon, a Jewish book not found in our Bibles today, expressed the popular opinion of the Messiah in Mary's day. Here are words from that text, so powerful and so evocative. Read them carefully, realize this was the popular view of the Messiah, and ask what Mary may have thought the Messiah would be like. If you want, compare these words with Mary's Magnificat. You might be surprised at the similarities.

First, the text of the *Psalms of Solomon* asserts that God will restore Israel *through a David-and-Solomon-like king, the Messiah.*

See, Lord, and raise up for them their king, the son of David, to rule over your servant Israel in the time known to you, O God. . . . [A]nd their king will be the Lord Messiah . . . for God made him powerful in the holy spirit and wise in the counsel of understanding, with strength and righteousness.

Second, this text also teaches that the Messiah will *drive Gentiles and sinners from the Land*:

Undergird him with the strength to destroy the unrighteous rulers, to purge Jerusalem from gentiles who trample her to destruction; in wisdom and in righteousness to drive out the sinners from the inheritance; to smash the arrogance of sinners like a potter's jar; to shatter their substance with an iron rod; to destroy the unlawful nations with the word of his mouth. . . .

Third, it also contends that the Messiah will *establish peace, righteousness, and holiness.*

He will gather a holy people whom he will lead in righteousness. . . . He will not tolerate unrighteousness (even) to pause among them, and any person who knows wickedness shall not live with them.

With these texts in mind, what do you think Mary thought of when she said "Messiah"? She certainly would have believed that God would bring victory—through the Messiah—over Gentiles like Herod Antipas and the new Roman emperor Tiberius. Also, she knew that God would banish sinners from the Land and would establish the reign of the Messiah to usher in peace for Israel. And at the bottom of it all, this Messiah, Mary knew, was her son.

Yet, Jesus did not seem to fit that script. Everyone, including Mary, was ambivalent about Jesus because he seemed to be reading a different Bible. I said earlier that Mary's problem was her interpretation of what the Bible predicted about the

Messiah. Her other problem was Jesus himself: He didn't act like the Messiah she (and everyone else) expected.

Ambivalence in Nazareth

The residents of Jesus' hometown, Nazareth, believed Jesus was an ordinary Jewish man. After hearing his first sermon in the synagogue, Mark's Gospel tells us, their question was, "Where did this man get these things?" They continued, "Isn't this the carpenter? Isn't this Mary's son and the brother of James, Joseph, Judas and Simon? Aren't his sisters here with us?" Then Mark adds in that same sixth chapter, "And they took offense at him." When Jesus claimed in that first sermon, as Luke 4 informs us, that Isaiah's words were coming true right then and there, the townsfolk of Nazareth couldn't believe that the Jesus they knew would make such a claim for himself. In their opinion, Jesus was just one of them.

He was. Yet, he wasn't. They certainly didn't believe God made himself human in the Jesus they witnessed. Jesus didn't scoot around Galilee two inches off the ground like a hover-craft. There was no halo—in spite of all the art that suggests differently—around his head for all to see his sanctity and saintliness. He grew up like other kids, he learned his spelling and arithmetic skills like other kids, and he didn't horse around by doing miracles.

It was difficult for some early Christians (and some today) to see Jesus as a real, normal human. We believe that Jesus was the God-man—both God and human at the same time. We're used to the belief that Jesus was the God-man, even though with a minute's serious thinking our brains do not grasp how this can be. Here's a good question if we want to understand how difficult it was for Mary to come to terms with who Jesus really was: What was it like for God to become a God-child? Surely, we say to ourselves, Jesus had to be different from the other kids. After all, how could a God-child be ordinary? We need to be real here, because if we are not careful, we'll be back singing that Christmas carol of that little "sweet head" and "no crying he makes." The tug we feel to make Jesus extraordinary is the same tug that pulled Mary into expecting Jesus to be super-extraordinary.

Without clear answers to some of the questions, some early Christians began filling in the gaps, imagining what it must have been like to be the God-child, and frankly just creating legends. A good example of such is the late second-century apocryphal *Infancy Gospel of Thomas*, which sensationalized the story of Jesus. As a five-year-old, this text tells us, Jesus was playing near a stream on a Sabbath. He gathered the water into small pools and then commanded them to become "clean" for ritual purposes. And they did. Then out of a water and dirt compound he made twelve mud sparrows. An observant Jew saw what he was doing, reported such to Joseph, and Joseph soon came to the scene to see what Jesus was doing. Joseph rebuked Jesus for his behavior, but Jesus responded by clapping his hands and speaking forth, "Be gone!" and the twelve sparrows flew away. People were amazed (as they no doubt would have been had Jesus actually done such things). In another story in the *Infancy Gospel of Thomas*, one man complained about Jesus and Jesus promptly made him wither up. A boy bumped into Jesus, so Jesus cursed him and the little boy died. The neighbors began to get worried. The text goes on in a similar manner.

Such a *Wunderkind* or, better yet what the French call an *enfant terrible*, Jesus was not. From every reliable account we have, Jesus was ordinary looking and ordinary acting. He may have been the Son of God, but the manner of being such a Son of God was not to dazzle, intimidate, or show off.

Which made Jesus' contemporaries, including Mary, ambivalent. There was a seemingly biblical script for the Messiah to dazzle, intimidate, and to show off, but Jesus didn't follow it. He should have been tall like Goliath and powerful like Saul and handsome like David and wise like Solomon—and carried around with him a little halo to make it indubitably obvious to everyone that he was the Messiah. But, that's not how God does things.

Mother of ambivalence

When Jesus was young and at home, Mary and Joseph could ponder their experiences with angels and relatives and shepherds and the Magi, and add them up to a dazzling Messianic display of glory. But once Jesus began his adult ministry, things changed—quickly. He followed a different biblical script. And Mary became ambivalent about Jesus: Was he the Messiah or not?

Here are the facts about Jesus' public ministry from the first three chapters of Mark's Gospel: Jesus exorcised demons, healed the sick, and restored lepers. Both to Mary and to the crowds, these actions seemed like early signs that Jesus was indeed the Messiah. But crowds were a concern to Rome, to Herod Antipas, and to the local Jewish leaders whose job it was to keep the peace. Was attracting crowds Messiah-like? Mary would have thought so. Jesus then claimed to forgive a paralyzed man's sins and proved his Messianic power by healing him and empowering him to walk. When the man danced home to tell everyone, trouble began to brew.

But then, as Mark's first few chapters record the facts, Jesus began to practice table fellowship many an evening with a motley band of tax collectors and sinners. "Why does he eat with tax collectors and sinners?" These words from Mark's second chapter are those of the Jewish leaders, but they were expressing what Mary and everyone else thought. Everyone knew the Messiah was to *purge* Israel of sinners, not *mix* with them.

Then, as we study Mark's second chapter, Jesus suggested that fasting was no longer necessary because the bridegroom had arrived for the banquet. Fasting, it needs to be observed, was a hallowed routine—twice a week for the pious. To suggest it could be dispensed with was impious. Next, Mark tells us that Jesus permitted his growing band of followers to pluck wheat and rub its grains loose, which is fine to do, except that he approved such behaviors for the Sabbath. This, too, violated sacred Sabbath customs for Jews.

All of this, Mark concludes, attracted ever bigger crowds, creating even more tension with the leaders. We should not be surprised that in the middle of all this, the leading lights for the pious, the Pharisees, "went out and began to plot with the Herodians how they might *kill* Jesus."

At this point you can understand why Mary grew ambivalent about Jesus. Messiahs who follow in the steps of Moses and David and Solomon and the prophets don't mix with sinners and they don't intentionally break Jewish laws and they don't flaunt Jewish piety and they don't teach their disciples to do the same. And Messiahs don't get themselves in trouble with the Jewish leadership. Messiahs may offend the Gentile rulers, but not the Jewish ones. A Messiah who acts like this just might not be the Messiah.

The script Mary envisioned for her messianic son and the script Jesus was following crashed like two rams battling for the higher ground. In Mark's third chapter we read about the scene this conflict created, a scene that proved to become a turning point in Mary's life: "When *his family* heard about [all] this [ministry], they went to take charge of him, for they said, *'He is out of his mind.'*" First, this is Jesus' *family*. Second, Jesus' family heard about his *ministry*—the material we sketched in the previous section—not only his scripted messianic miracles and teachings but also his mixing with sinners and conflicting with leaders. The family, with Mary at the helm, came to the conclusion that Jesus was *out of his mind*, that Jesus had gotten his messianic mission all wrong, that this Son of the Father was not really listening to the Father. Maybe, Mary must have been thinking, Jesus wasn't the Messiah. Maybe he needed some help from his mother.

The family heard about Jesus' ministry while they were up in Nazareth. From there, Mary pulled her children in tow, headed for Capernaum, resolutely determined to get to Jesus to talk sense into him. If Mary didn't get to him, she realized, the authorities would, and they'd put Jesus to death for breaking the Sabbath and claiming to forgive sins and flaunting Jewish observance. For the real Mary, it was that serious. Mary's ambivalence is clear: She believed her son was the promised Messiah and, at the same time, she knew what he was doing was contrary to what the Messiah was promised to do. Something had to change.

So Mary left home, made the trip over to the Sea of Galilee, asked questions, and discovered Jesus' location. She found Jesus in a home, once again in the middle of a circle with folks listening to his wisdom. The scene reminds us of the Passover, when Jesus was twelve. And his response to her this time was not unlike the response then.

In the last paragraph of his third chapter, Mark tells us that "Jesus' mother and brothers arrived" at the house in Capernaum. When Jesus heard that they were at the door, his question was not what one would have expected from a Jewish son intent on observing the Fifth Commandment to honor his mother. But it was the sort of thing Jesus was famous for: "Who," Jesus asks in the face of his mother and siblings, "are my mother and my brothers?" Then he looked at those seated in a circle around him [his disciples] and said, "Here are my mother and my brothers! Whoever does God's will is my brother and sister and mother."

In front of his mother and family Jesus publicly identified his family as those who do the will of his Father and thereby made it potently clear that his mission was to create a new family. Instead of reestablishing a physical Davidic dynasty as Mary believed he would, Jesus was establishing a "dynasty" of another sort: Jesus was creating a family based on following Jesus, the family of the faithful, the family of his Father. Jesus revealed to Mary that the Messiah's task was to create a new family, centered around him, and anyone desiring to do God's will would have to enter into this new circle of faith. Mary was no exception.

These were harsh words for a woman who showed such zeal for the Messiah and who showed such *chutzpah* as did Mary. These were harsh words for a mother who had charged down from Nazareth to rescue Jesus from those who might seek his death. These were harsh words for someone who thought she had the term "Messiah" figured out.

Mary came to Capernaum to rescue Jesus. What she got instead was a lesson about the meaning of Messiah, and before she walked out the door that day she would have to make her decision. She would have to decide if Jesus was really the Messiah or not. She would have to decide whether to follow him and join his new family.

At the very center of Jesus' mission for Mary was the summons to leave the honor code of the Fifth Commandment and to follow him as the Lord of a new family of faith. What he said when his mother came to that doorway he said in other ways at other times. Notice two examples of similar pronouncements by Jesus, and imagine hearing them as Mary heard them. The first is from Mark's tenth chapter:

> "Truly I tell you," Jesus replied, "no one who has left home or brothers or sisters or mother or father or children or fields for me and the gospel will fail to receive a hundred times as much in this present age: homes, brothers, sisters, mothers, children and fields—along with persecutions—and in the age to come eternal life. But many who are first will be last, and the last first."

The second is from the tenth chapter of Matthew:

Do not suppose that I have come to bring peace to the earth. I did not come to bring peace, but a sword. For I have come to turn

a man against his father,
a daughter against her mother,
a daughter-in-law against her mother-in-law—
your enemies will be the members of your own household.

It's not recorded that Mary ever heard Jesus say these words, but I suspect she did. These sharp words of Jesus pierced her soul because they were words reflecting Jesus' own experience of family rejection. And, as he summoned his followers to endure that kind of rejection, so he pressed home to his mother that she, too, would have to follow him. The Father's family, he said to her, does God's will by sitting at my feet and following me, by listening to my words and putting them into practice.

Family ambivalence

Jesus summoned all, including his mother, to join his Father's family. His new family had one characteristic: obedience. Connection in this family wasn't genetic. The characteristic of Jesus' family was surrendering in faith to him. "Do whatever he tells you" was the motto and mantra of Jesus' new family of disciples. How did Mary respond?

In spite of the intensity of the scene at Capernaum, we do not again hear about Mary until we find her looking at Jesus when he was crucified. Do we believe that Mary did not enter into the

Father's family when Jesus confronted her in Capernaum? It is unreasonable to think she walked away. Mary had heard Gabriel, she had heard Elizabeth, she had heard the prophetic words of Simeon and Anna, and she had heard from the shepherds and the Magi. And then, as if observing her son blossom from a messianic bud, she watched her son's powerfully effective ministry. Isn't it more likely to think that Mary showed the same character she had shown before and uttered yet one more "may it be" or a "do whatever he tells you"?

While the Gospels are silent about Mary for the rest of Jesus' ministry, what we do know is that Mary was at the crucifixion scene and that, after the resurrection and ascension of Jesus, she was in the middle of the apostolic band gathered at the Day of Pentecost. It simply makes logical sense to think Mary responded as she always had: Not only did she honor Jesus as her Lord, but she most likely also joined the new family of Jesus at that time.

We can understand Mary's struggle. No one, including Mary, anticipated the kind of Messiah Jesus would become. Following Jesus proved as difficult for Mary as for Peter and for John the Baptist (who himself had plenty of ambivalence about Jesus) and for the siblings of Jesus. Mary's special challenge was to trust that the God who spoke to her in and through the Magnificat was at work in Jesus in his ministry and his mission. While the two visions of the Messiah—the one in the Magnificat and the one guiding Jesus' public ministry—didn't seem to fit, it was hers to trust that Jesus really was the Messiah.

The next time we see Mary, she will be standing at the cross during the Jewish observance of Passover watching her son being tortured by the Roman soldiers. Mary learned that there was another way to read the Bible's vision of the Messiah. There was the Messianic theme of victory and triumph, and there was the Messianic theme of suffering with others, instead of others, and on behalf of others. Suffering for others was a theme written into the very fabric of Jewish life, for the Passover observance itself revealed a lamb was to be slain to liberate the children of God. The final lesson Mary would learn was that the Passover blood would be Jesus' own blood: He would die for others in order to form a new family of faith.

Jesus' death would become the scandal of the Christian gospel. This scandal was the biggest challenge she and any Jewish follower of Jesus would encounter. The real Jesus would be a crucified Messiah. Simeon's sword would finally pierce Mary's soul.

10

" Near the cross of Jesus stood his mother"

WOMAN OF FAITHFULNESS

Mary disappears from the Gospel stories after the incident at the doorway in Capernaum, and we don't see her again until the life of her son is coming to a close. We find her at the crucifixion of Jesus. Mary, the mother of the one being crucified, stood near the cross. She observed the barbaric scene with the beloved disciple John and with some of her friends who were also disciples of Jesus.

Here's the bare record of the fact of Mary's presence in John's Gospel, a fact not found in Matthew or in Mark or in Luke. Only John's nineteenth chapter tells us that Mary was at the cross.

Near the cross of Jesus stood his mother, his mother's sister, Mary the wife of Clopas, and Mary Magdalene. When Jesus saw his mother there, and the disciple whom he loved standing nearby, he said to her, "Woman, here is your son," and to the disciple, "Here is your mother." From that time on, this disciple took her into his home.

If it has been a challenge for us up to this point to enter into the real Mary's life to understand how she responded to her son's messianic *vocation*, it is beyond a challenge to imagine her thoughts as she watched her son suffer at the cross.

The real Mary, a disciple of her own son and in the "new family" he had formed, stood near the cross. From the comforts of air-conditioned and heated churches we sing *The Old Rugged Cross* or *The Ballad of the Cross* and remember, sometimes only romantically, what God did for us. But, the real Mary heard the thud of pounding nails and the sounds of piercing pain. Mary barely comprehended that it was for her that her son died. But she stood near the cross as an act of faithful allegiance to her son, and the real Mary embraced the real cross—as her son writhed on it.

It is one thing to be a follower of Jesus; it was another to follow Jesus as his life rolled into the unknown future. Mary was that kind of follower.

Faithfulness at the cross

Mary stood with three friends, two of whom were named "Mary," something that should not surprise us since about fifty percent of Jewish women in the first century had that name.

First was Mary's sister, *Salome*—who happens to be the mother of the apostles James and John. Second, *Mary, wife of Clopas*, about whom we know nothing. Third, *Mary Magdalene*, the one from whom Jesus had exorcised seven demons.

Some of Mary's friends, as we learn from the first few lines in Luke's eighth chapter, followed Jesus throughout his Galilean ministry and routinely cooked and provided essentials for Jesus and his disciples. The fifteenth chapter of Mark's Gospel has a parallel to the lines we quoted above from John's nineteenth chapter about the women at the crucifixion scene: In "Galilee these women had *followed* him and *cared for his needs*." The women at the cross, including Mary, were disciples of Jesus, not spectators. Mary's presence at the cross involved more than motherly care for a son. These women stood near the cross because they were disciples.

What strikes us today is that Mary and other women disciples were at the cross while the male disciples of Jesus fled—all of them—except the beloved disciple, John, son of Zebedee and Salome. In our reading of the Gospel records, it is reasonable to conjecture that the disciples who fled were failing in their faith, while Mary, the beloved disciple, and the other women remained faithful. Another reading proves just as reasonable, namely that the male disciples fled because they were the same kind of threat to the leaders that Jesus was, while the women disciples were not. In this reading, the beloved disciple may have been too young to threaten the authorities. We might want to factor both of these views into our understanding of Mary's presence at the scene—the males were a threat and were afraid, while the women were not so much a threat and were not afraid. However we put it together, these *women disciples remained faithful to Jesus during the crucifixion.*

Mary was faithful to her son—as son and as Lord—even if it meant absorbing the humiliation of the crucifixion. Mary's faithfulness derives from her conviction that Jesus, *in spite* of the cross, was the Messiah, and her conviction that God, *in spite* of this turn of events, was in control. Mary would remain faithful to Jesus through this rugged scene and through two dark days of wondering, and then beyond those right through to Easter morning. Once Jesus was raised from the dead, Mary's faithfulness at the cross would blossom into the conviction that God's redemptive work had occurred when she, with her friends, stood with tears in their eyes near the cross of Jesus.

At the moment, though, the cross was a blatant act of violent death for her son.

The scene was gruesome. The authorities, both Jewish and Roman, interviewed Jesus in a series of trials. Jesus slept little, if at all. The soldiers humiliated him and punished his body. He carried the cross in the hot, morning sun to Golgotha. They hoisted the cross up so that it could fall into the hole they dug for it. When that cross struck the bottom after being dropped into the hole, the tendons and ligaments in the joints of Jesus' hands, wrists, and feet stretched and tore. Jesus was bleeding and thirsty and dying the slow death of asphyxiation.

For any of us, it is nearly impossible to take this in. How did Mary handle this? Was she tempted to become ambivalent about this Messiah again? Did she think that this might be the end of the story of her son? Nothing indicates her ambivalence at the cross. Was she not aware that Jesus had predicted both this gruesome death *and* a resurrection of victory beyond the grave? After all, Jesus had said more than one time that he would not only die in Jerusalem but he would be raised—such predictions are found in Mark's central chapters (8, 9, and 10).

Even if she was aware that this was Good Friday and that Easter was on its way, the scene was gruesome and she felt pain. Was this the sword Simeon predicted? For the real Mary, the cross was real. I wonder sometimes what Mary would think of Christians wearing a cross around the neck. Would she think a diamond-laced cross appropriate? Would she think a shiny cross something Christian? So used to it are we that we rarely pause to think what we are wearing. A cross was a brutal instrument used by brutal leaders to scare everyone into submission and to wreak vengeance on enemies of the State. Mary knew what the cross was really like, and learning to see a cross around the neck through Mary's eyes might help us realize what we are wearing. We can be sure of this: The cross Mary saw was brutal.

Faithfulness from the cross

Mary's faithfulness to Jesus when he was on the cross mirrors Jesus' own faithfulness to her from the cross.

As he hung there on the cross, Jesus did what the observant and pious Jew was supposed to do: He provided a "last will and testament" for his mother. His words, said to Mary and John, were "Woman [or, Mother], here is your son." To the beloved disciple, who was a cousin, Jesus said: "Here is your mother." Mary experienced this transfer to John's family as a form of double honor. He cared for her as his mother and he also secured her place in his new family of the Father.

Jesus had used some distancing words with his mother at times, both at the wedding at Cana and when Mary and Jesus' brothers and sisters came to Capernaum to protect him from danger. Mary responded to God in each of these circumstances as she should have, and that is why viewing Mary at the cross as a disciple of Jesus explains so much. As she stood near the cross, she received a double reward for following him: Jesus honored her both as his mother *and* as member of his family of faith. The distance is over because Mary has crossed the threshold to embrace Jesus as Lord. She is his mother—and he acknowledges that—and she is also his disciple—and he acknowledges that, too.

But there is a quiet tragedy here for Mary. What an ordinary observer of this crucifixion scene expects is for Jesus to commit Mary to her other children, to one of Jesus' younger brothers. But he doesn't do that. Mary finds herself between families: Her primary caregiver, Jesus—because Joseph is presumed deceased—is about to die. Where will she go home now? Why doesn't Jesus commit her to his siblings? There is evidence that the brothers of Jesus did not think he was the Messiah. John's seventh chapter tells us that "even his own brothers did not believe in him." The most reasonable explanation, then, for why Mary is committed to John instead of to one of Jesus' siblings emerges from the tragic reality, weighing no doubt on Mary herself, that they did not yet believe in Jesus.

Jesus had transferred Mary to a new family, but moving in with John involved experiencing the pain of the cross, the pain of family division that Jesus himself had spoken of so frequently. Mary, it can be said, experienced the cross at the cross.

Faithfulness of God in the cross

This book has explained how the real Mary came to terms (as any ordinary Jew would have had to) with the messianic vocation of Jesus, even though we can be sure she did not fully come to terms with Jesus' mission until after the Resurrection and Pentecost. With the New Testament Scriptures already tucked away in our minds, it is easy for us to sit in judgment of Mary and think of Jesus' mission as an obvious mission to die (a cross-vocation). But very little in the Jewish world would have helped Mary to expect the Messiah to die for sins on a cross. *Nothing* in the Jewish literature at the time of Jesus gives us the impression that Jews thought the Messiah would die for sins as a sacrifice. Sacrifice took place in the Temple using innocent animals; Messiahs don't die as sacrifices.

As Christians, we have learned to read the Bible as signposts pointing to Jesus' death, and we have learned to think of the Messiah through the lens of Isaiah's great servant passage in chapters fifty-two and fifty-three. We think of these words:

See, my servant will act wisely;
> he will be raised and lifted up and highly exalted.
> Just as there were many who were appalled at him—
his appearance was so disfigured beyond that of any human being
and his form marred beyond human likeness—

But neither Mary nor the disciples thought of those verses as the Messiah's task. And we think of these words too:

He was oppressed and afflicted,
      yet he did not open his mouth;
      he was led like a lamb to the slaughter,
            and as a sheep before its shearers is silent,
            so he did not open his mouth.

But, again, that is not the passage Mary would have turned to when she pondered prophecies of the Messiah. Nor did she think of these words:

He was assigned a grave with the wicked,
      and with the rich in his death,
      though he had done no violence,
            nor was any deceit in his mouth.
Yet it was the LORD'S will to crush him and cause him to suffer,
      and though the LORD makes his life an offering for sin,

Nor these:

Therefore I will give him a portion among the great,
      and he will divide the spoils with the strong,
because he poured out his life unto death,
      and was numbered with the transgressors.
For he bore the sin of many,
      and made intercession for the transgressors.

Mary and her contemporaries thought of the Messiah as a powerful Davidic king sitting atop a throne in Jerusalem, triumphantly routing the Gentiles, conquering the Land, and guiding everyone in wisdom to observe the Torah. Embracing a Messiah who would make death on a cross central to his role challenged Mary's faithfulness more than anything she would face.

The story not told in books about Mary is that she, like everyone else, had to learn to read the Bible in a new way. She had to learn that the Messiah's task was to bring redemption and justice *through death on the cross,* and that through that death he would create a new family where justice and peace would take root through self-sacrificing love. She had to learn that God expressed his own covenant faithfulness to redeem his people when he sent his Son to die for us.

On that last day, when the real Mary stared at the cross with Jesus, the Messiah—indeed, her Messiah, hanging on it, Mary began to realize not only what Simeon's "sword" meant but also how God planned to make the Magnificat real. Mary would soon comprehend—and it would be after Pentecost when this became clear to her—that the political and dynastic hope for triumph over the enemies, the yearning for routing unjust rulers, and the lingering sense of a powerful vindication for the poor fell in folds at her feet along with the clothing of Jesus.

Jesus would not wear the crown of Caesar Augustus or the fine apparel of Herod Antipas. He would hang there, naked and beaten, and give to Mary and the world a radically new view of what it means to reign in this world. To reign in this world, Mary began to learn, was to give one's life for others as Jesus had given his.

The real John who stood next to the real Mary that day near the cross and who took her into his home, would later remember what Jesus had said on the last night he spent with his family of faith: "Greater love has no one than this: to lay down one's life for one's friends." This from the fifteenth chapter of his Gospel. In the third chapter of his first letter he will eventually write this: "This is how we know what love is: Jesus Christ laid down his life for us. And we ought to lay down our lives for one another." Is it possible for Mary to have lived in John's home until the end of her life and not have shared similar thoughts?

Three days after Jesus' death on the cross the followers of Jesus began to tell a new story: *Easter*. Mary was there, and as indicated above, Easter transformed Mary's perception of that awful day when she watched her son's public, humiliating crucifixion. She saw him die, and then she heard the reports that he was alive again, though there is no record that Jesus ever appeared to her personally.

Fifty days after the Passover feast at which Jesus died, we find yet another story: *Pentecost*. On that day, the followers of Jesus gathered in Jerusalem for yet one more Jewish feast, Pentecost. In the middle of those followers was Mary (and Jesus' brothers, we should note). On that day they gathered to pray, and once again something surprising happened: The long-awaited day of the Spirit's coming swooped down from heaven, flooded them with spiritual strength, and empowered them to declare the gospel of Jesus Christ—the one who died and the one who was raised from the dead. Luke, the author of the Acts of the Apostles, does not say much about Mary, but he does tell us that she was present when this climactic event occurred.

Even if Mary did not at first realize it, Pentecost brought all of God's promises to her together: The Magnificat's dream of a society governed by justice with peace streaming through its streets would come through the paradox of the Cross, the power of the Resurrection, and the life-giving creativity of the gift of the Spirit of God. The society of the Magnificat that Mary anticipated from the day Gabriel revealed it to her would come to pass in the Church. And in the middle of these church cells in Jerusalem was Mary.

The story of Mary in the New Testament ends with Mary in the middle of a confident, growing, and discovering Christian community in Jerusalem that was finding its way without Jesus physically present, now guided by the Holy Spirit, with everything in the world to look forward to. The story I have told about Mary is the story of the real Mary. It is a story that has rarely been told.

But we have not finished: Mary's story, much of it never told, generated yet more stories about Mary—stories that grievously have divided Christians for hundreds of years. They, too, are part of the story of Mary—and it will be up to each of us to decide if they are part of the story of the *real* Mary or not.

part II
The Ongoing Life of Mary in the Church

11

"Along with the women and Mary, mother of Jesus"

WOMAN OF INFLUENCE

We have one more line in the New Testament about Mary to explore, and I will suggest in this chapter that this line tells the story of Mary's powerful influence in the earliest Church. In the first chapter of Acts, after Jesus had ascended and the disciples had gathered together in Jerusalem at the Feast of Pentecost, we are told of those who were present in that first new family of God: "They all joined together constantly in prayer, along with the women *and Mary mother of Jesus*, and with his brothers."

What this text tells us is that Mary was present in the inner circle of the new family of God. This small circle had come through the whole story: They knew Jesus before the cross, at the cross, and beyond the cross. By sitting in this circle a little more than a month after Jesus' death and resurrection, every person publicly confessed a Messiah who was crucified and raised. Mary was in the middle of the family of Jesus.

What was her role in that new family?

I want to suggest that Mary exercised influence from the Church's very beginning, and that influence was manifested in several ways. I begin with her own sons. For some, this may come as a surprise, and for others it will be non-news. Why? Roman Catholics firmly believe that Mary had no children of her own after she gave birth to Jesus, and Protestants have always assumed that Mary and Joseph had other children because that is how we have learned to interpret the biblical text when it speaks of Jesus' "brothers and sisters." Catholics read "brothers and sisters" as either "cousins" or relatives." At the end of this chapter I will sketch my reasons for believing Mary and Joseph had other children.

Mary's influence on Jesus and James

Some of us are not realistic when it comes to looking into Jesus' own development. As a result, we miss observing the influence of his earthly father and mother. (This is not to rule out the Son's eternal and personal relationship with his heavenly Father.) After Mary and Joseph returned to Nazareth, Luke's second chapter tells us, Jesus "grew and became strong; he was filled with wisdom, and the grace of God was on him." Luke tells us at the end of that chapter that when the holy family got back to Nazareth after Jesus' little incident in the Temple, Jesus "grew up" and "he increased in wisdom and in favor with God and people."

Jesus learned his ABCs—in Hebrew his *aleph, bet, gimels*—and his math problems and he learned how to speak and write as any Jewish boy would have learned—from his parents. I sometimes hear Christians suggest that Jesus was inordinately precocious, knowing everything at birth and needing no instruction. Yet, this isn't what the Bible says. The Gospel of Luke says that Jesus grew and developed. Christian theology has always taught that Jesus was fully God and fully human as the God-man. If Jesus was fully human, he grew as we grow, he learned as we learn, and he developed as we develop. And we learn much of what we learn from our parents.

Which means that, in the real world, Joseph and Mary had a significant influence on the real Jesus.

We don't know enough about Joseph to know what he would have taught Jesus other than the norm—how to hunt, how to fish, how to chip wood, and how to lay the foundation for a wall. But, because Joseph was known according to Matthew's first chapter as a "righteous" man (a *tsadiq*), we can also be sure that Joseph taught Jesus the ins and outs of the Torah.

We know much more about Mary, and so it is important that we consider the influence of Mary on Jesus. We can return once again to the Magnificat, for here we find uncanny similarities between what God revealed through Mary and the central themes of Jesus' mission. Here's the question I'd like you to ask as you consider the evidence below: Where do you think Jesus learned these things?

First, as Mary exclaimed "holy is his name," *so Jesus* taught his followers to pray to the Father, "hallowed [holy] be your name." Second, as Mary gloried in the arrival of food, the relief of poverty, and the elevation of those who were oppressed when she proclaimed, "he has filled the hungry with good things," *so her son* blessed the poor and fed the hungry. Third, as Mary saw God at work bringing "down rulers from their thrones," *so Jesus* regularly had strong words with political and religious leaders about injustice and corruption. Fourth, as Mary knew the mercy of God for herself, for her relative Elizabeth, and for her people Israel, *so Jesus* became famous for his deeds of mercy and acts of compassion. Fifth, as Mary yearned for the redemption of Israel, like Simeon and Anna and all the other *Anawim* (righteous poor), *so Jesus' heart* was broken over the condition of Israel, and he longed for it to return as a chicken brood to its mother. Finally, as Mary herself almost certainly became a widow, *so Jesus* himself regularly went out of his way to care for widows in their distress.

Isn't it likely that some of these themes in the ministry of Jesus were shaped by his mother? The real Jesus learned things from the real Mary. She influenced Jesus and taught him in the way of the Magnificat. She did what mothers have always done: She taught her son the ways of God.

One could easily extend these observations to the similarities between Mary's Magnificat, her own Magna Carta, and the themes of another son, James. Sometime read the Magnificat quickly and then read the letter of James quickly. You'll notice at least the following similarities, and if we want to know about the real Mary and the real James, it is worth our time to ask if some of this is a family connection. Surely one sees such potential influence of Mary in James' blessing of the poor and then his stiff warnings for the rich and his call to care for widows, as well as in his emphasis on mercy, faith, humility, peace, and wisdom. But, when in James' letter he quotes Proverbs 3:34 in his fourth chapter, saying that "God opposes the proud but shows favor to the humble and oppressed," and then goes on to say, "Humble yourselves before the LORD, and he will lift you up," he's reintroducing pure Magnificat. This is probably the message he heard at home his entire life.

If we simply grant that Mary was involved in teaching and modeling godly behavior before her children, we are justified in finding influences of Mary in the teachings of both Jesus and James. The real Mary, I am suggesting, was an influential woman.

Mary's influential presence in the New Testament

Mary stands out from the ordinary among the followers of Jesus. Sometimes it is said that Mary rarely appears in the earliest Christian sources. I'm not so sure it would be fair to say Mary is a marginal character in the early Christian story.

Let's briefly review what the Bible says about Mary.

- Mary appeared everywhere in the first two chapters of both the Gospels of Luke and Matthew, the infancy narratives in our Gospels.

- She was a central character in the wedding at Cana.

- She led her family down to Capernaum from Nazareth and knocked on the door one time where Jesus was speaking, and Jesus put her off for the moment.

- Her son was referred to as the "son of Mary" by the local townspeople in Nazareth when Jesus taught spectacularly at the synagogue. ("Son of Mary" was a slur on Jesus' presumed illegitimacy.)

- One time a woman blessed Mary, and Jesus replied, "Blessed rather are those who hear the word of God and obey it" (Luke 11:27-28).

- At his crucifixion, Jesus appointed the apostle John, the beloved disciple, to care for his mother. Then John says this: "From that time on, this disciple took her into his home."

- After Jesus' death and resurrection, Mary is mentioned as being present when the early leaders of the new family of Jesus gathered to pray and when the Spirit came at Pentecost.

- In the fourth chapter of Galatians Paul mentions that Jesus was "born of a woman."

- Some have argued that the woman of Revelation 12 is actually Mary. (While I disagree, we'll look at this passage in the next chapter.)

Added up, there are more than a dozen instances of Mary's being mentioned, either in passing or at length, in the New Testament. There are approximately 217 verses in the New Testament in which Mary plays a part. If we compare Mary to other figures, other than Peter and Paul and John, she survives the comparison well.

Mary's influence in the earliest churches

Mary was the only one who knew some facts about Jesus. She and God and Joseph (because the angel told him) were the only ones who knew about the virginal conception. She was either the only one present or one of the few present when Gabriel spoke, when Elizabeth exclaimed her joy about Mary's child, when Mary sang the Magnificat, and when Simeon and Anna prophesied. She was one of two present when the shepherds announced their good news and when the Magi offered gifts to Jesus, the newborn king. She was one of the few who knew about the wine at Cana, and she was one of the few who heard Jesus speak from the cross. So, when it is argued that the Gospels are in part Mary's "memoirs," we must agree with the general drift: For from whom else would the early Christians—and the Evangelists—have learned about these things if not from Mary?

There are good reasons for Luke to tell us that Mary spent significant time pondering the story of Jesus. There are good reasons for us to think that Mary not only pondered that story but also passed it on. At the very least, Mary was justifiably proud of her son—who wouldn't be proud to be the mother of the Messiah? In a real world, mothers tell stories about their sons. Mary did too. In order to compose a true account about Jesus, the Evangelists and other early Christians would have sought out Mary to ask what Jesus was like, to ask what he said and to whom and why. She was in the middle of the earliest Christian community as a source of information about Jesus.

When Luke tells us in the first chapter of Acts that the apostles of Jesus had returned to Jerusalem and that "they all joined together constantly in prayer, along with the women and Mary the mother of Jesus, and with his brothers," who was there? The apostles. And with the apostles were women, *Mary*, and Jesus' brothers. Luke tells us there were only about one hundred and twenty believers present.

To mention Mary, along with the brothers of Jesus, is an indicator of her importance to that first gathering of the followers of Jesus. We never hear about her again in the pages of the New Testament, but we can be sure that she continued to be the woman she had been: courageous, dangerous, faithful, assertive, and hopeful for the kingdom of God.

What we know is that Mary partook in the prayers of that community, she participated in the gift of tongues at Pentecost, and she was surely part of the groundswell of those first active apostolic church gatherings. Remember that Jesus handed Mary over to his cousin John. And John, if we also remember, was a significant leader in the first churches in Jerusalem. If Mary stayed with John, Mary was part of those first communities.

And this, as recorded in Acts 2, is what she would have witnessed:

They [including Mary] devoted themselves to the apostles' teaching and to fellowship, to the breaking of bread and to prayer. Everyone was filled with awe at the many wonders and signs performed by the apostles. All the believers were together and had everything in common. They sold property and possessions to give to anyone who had need. Every day they continued to meet together in the temple courts. They broke bread in their homes and ate together with glad and sincere hearts, praising God and enjoying the favor of all the people. And the Lord added to their number daily those who were being saved.

In fact, it is not hard to connect the dots between Mary's Magnificat, Jesus' teachings on the kingdom in the Gospel of Luke (chapters four, six, and seven) about the kingdom of God, and these little economically sharing and mutually responsible house churches in Jerusalem. God's kingdom would recreate society through a relationship with Jesus by forming a new family that would live according to God's will. This early Jerusalem's community life of sharing everything in common fulfills what Mary predicted in the Magnificat when she announced that the poor would have their needs taken care of. In connecting these passages, I am suggesting she exercised influence in those early communities.

We should be cautious—but not skeptical—about the influence of Mary on Jesus, James, and the early Christian churches.

Mary, Joseph, Sex, and Siblings

We have done our best to avoid the entangling debates between Protestants and Roman Catholic teachings about Mary. But let's explore one such debate and, once again to speak realistically, look at Mary's sexual relations with Joseph. If she did have sexual relations with Joseph, something that seems likely, then the very names of her sons may lend some clues about Mary's influence.

Did Mary have children after Jesus? With very few exceptions, all Christians from the second or third century onwards believed that Mary was perpetually virginal. That is, not only did she conceive as a virgin, she was (as an early creed has it) "ever-virgin." Which means, just in case we need to fill in the lines, that she and Joseph lived together as husband and wife without sexual relations. This surprises many of us. What may surprise us even more is that three of the most significant Protestant leaders—Martin Luther, John Calvin, and John Wesley—who in their own way were also very critical of what Catholics believed about Mary, each believed in Mary's perpetual virginity.

If Joseph and Mary did not have sexual relations, why—some Protestants may ask—didn't they? While other possible explanations have been given for this, the standard response is that both Joseph and Mary knew the sacredness of Mary's womb as a result of having carried the Son of God, and that awareness alone led them to think sexual relations would be inappropriate.

Well, was she perpetually a virgin? There are two major reasons why many Protestants—and we have shifted considerably on this issue since the days of those early leaders—maintain that Mary and Joseph had normal sexual relations and had children. First, Matthew 1:25 says that Joseph "had no union with her [Mary] *until* she gave birth to a son." It is possible that Joseph had no union "until" they were married as well as "after" they were married. But, in nearly all of the cases when this expression "until" is used there is a change of conditions after the "until." So, there is a presumption in favor of *until* meaning that Joseph and Mary did have sexual relations after Jesus' birth.

Second, and more important, the New Testament regularly tells us that Jesus had "brothers" and "sisters." While it is true that both of these terms can refer to cousins, relatives, half-siblings and step-siblings, the normal meaning of *brother* and *sister* is *blood-brother/sister*. A standard rule of interpretation is that words carry normal meanings unless the context suggests otherwise. Here is my own conclusion—and I share this with the majority of Protestant interpreters: There is nothing in any of the contexts when Jesus' brothers and sisters are mentioned to suggest that the words mean anything other than blood-brother and blood-sister.

I join the current majority Protestant view on this issue: It is highly probable that Mary and Joseph had normal sexual relations and that the "brothers" and "sisters" of Jesus were his younger siblings. If this is the case, then the names of Jesus' brothers tell a story.

Mary's evocation with names
Back up to the Gospel of Mark, chapter 6, verse 3. Here are the names of Jesus' brothers given in that text: "James, Joseph, Judas, and Simon." If we translate those names into Hebrew, they would be *Yakov, Yoseph, Yehudah, and Shimeon.* Let's put a few clear facts together. The first one is that Mary and Joseph, not long after the birth of Jesus, were warned by an angel to flee to Egypt. A second factor to consider is that the biblical account of the children of Israel in Egypt includes the blessing of Jacob (*Yakov*) on his twelve sons, three of whom were named *Yoseph, Yehudah,* and *Shimeon.* I suggest that the choice of these names by Joseph and Mary tells us something very significant about Mary. To anticipate what we will lay out in the barest of details, our conclusion will be this: In Egypt, Joseph and Mary named

their sons *Yakov, Yoseph, Yehudah, and Shimeon* in order to evoke the conviction that God would liberate Israel from Rome and would give to Israel new "tribal" leaders. I emphasize that this is a suggestion.

Let me now lay out the facts and then put them together in such a way that reveals my hypothesis that the names of Jesus' siblings evoked the theme of liberation and the creation of a new Israel. We should recall that Jacob, also called Israel, had twelve sons. One of them was Joseph, who became the prince of Egypt and who attracted his brothers to Egypt. Over time, these sons—by now called the "children of Israel"—were enslaved in Egypt and longed to return to the Land. God entered the picture at this point and worked a miracle—at Passover God liberated Israel from Pharaoh and Israel returned (after forty years of wandering in the desert) to the Land, where they established a twelve-tribe nation.

Now enter Joseph and Mary. They, too, were sojourning in Egypt and they, too, longed to return. Here is my contention: Joseph and Mary named their boys, perhaps when they were in Egypt or perhaps after they returned, *Yakov, Yoseph, Yehudah, and Shimeon*. Each of these names, however common, derives from the tribal leaders of Israel. My suggestion then is this: Mary and Joseph named their sons after those leaders in order to express their hope that God would free Israel from Rome and establish their son, Jesus, and his brothers as the new leaders for Israel. I consider this as a possibility. Mary and Joseph gave their boys names that evoke the dream of God liberating Israel from oppression. You make up your own mind.

Whether you join me or not in this suggestion, there is no doubt that Mary, the mother of Jesus, was an influential woman in her immediate family (with Jesus and James) and in the earliest Christian family sitting in a circle around Jesus. Take this chapter as an evangelical Protestant's commitment to the Bible and his exploration of Mary's influence. Let us now consider how the real Mary's life exerted much more influence, as we will soon see, in the history of the Church.

12

Protestants, Roman Catholics, and Mary

WOMAN OF CONTROVERSY 1: *The Early Developments*

After the crucifixion, Mary appears in the first chapter of the Acts of the Apostles. We don't learn much, but what we learn is significant: She was part of the earliest devoted followers of Jesus who gathered together on the Day of Pentecost to pray. And their prayers were surely answered—for the Spirit swooped down and carried the earliest followers of Jesus into a history that is ongoing to this very day. That Mary was part of this small clutch of followers of Jesus informs us that Mary embraced the cross as the work of God and understood that cross in light of the Resurrection.

•

Pentecost, however, is the last word we hear about Mary in the New Testament.

But what happened to Mary after Pentecost? We really don't know. Yet, more so for Mary than for any other person in the New Testament, Christians throughout almost two thousand years of Church history have been compelled to fill in the gaps of what we do not know about Mary. That story, should one be interested, has been wonderfully told by the late Yale theologian Jaroslav Pelikan in his book *Mary through the Centuries.*

The story of Mary has continually developed in the story-telling of the universal Church, though its development in the Roman Catholic Church and the Eastern Orthodox Church outstrips anything Protestants have said. In fact, Protestants have spent some of their time arguing against most of the developments about Mary in the Catholic and Orthodox traditions. In chapter eleven we began to look at this ongoing story about Mary.

Now we'll look at the major ideas about Mary that have developed in the Church, especially the Roman Catholic Church. Whether or not we agree with our Roman Catholic friends when it comes to Mary, we might at least inform ourselves of what other branches of the Church believe so that we can converse with one another respectfully and intelligently—and we already know that at times our responses to one another have been little more than knee-jerk reactions.

Let's begin with the major similarity between Protestants and Catholics: We both believe in the supernatural conception of Jesus. This permits us to join hands on a very significant doctrine of the Christian faith. Howard Marshall, a well-known evangelical New Testament scholar, expresses himself this way about the miraculous conception of Jesus: "In the end, it is a question of whether we are prepared to believe in the creative power of the Spirit of God. . . ." Together, Roman Catholics and many Protestants are not only prepared to believe but really do believe in the virginal conception as a result of God's creative Spirit.

Some are surprised about even more similarities: There is what I call a growing "Mariaphilia"—a growing love of Mary by Protestants. No one reveals this trend more than Tim Perry, professor of theology at Providence College, a Christian college in Canada. In his new book, *Mary for Evangelicals*, Tim presents what can only be called an evangelical "theology of Mary." His book illustrates that for many the Cold War between Catholics and Protestants over Mary has come to an end. And agreement is beginning to extend well beyond the teachings about the virginal conception.

We can't be fair to this discussion unless we also bring to the table The Big Difference: Protestants limit their theology as much as possible to the Bible. Roman Catholics anchor their beliefs in both the Bible and the ongoing, developing sacred Tradition. There is no getting around it: Every discussion between Protestants and Catholics eventually ends up with the two facing the question of the role of Tradition.

But we Protestants should know this: No Roman Catholic is bothered by the routine Protestant accusation that what they believe about Mary can't be found in the New Testament. They already know that, and it doesn't faze them. What Roman Catholics believe is that the New Testament images of Mary, which we have sketched in the previous eleven chapters, are like an origami figure that has been unfolded in Church traditions for nearly two thousand years, and each unfolding leads to yet more insights into Mary. Roman Catholics refer to the New Testament images and their developments in Tradition as the *real* Mary.

We focus in what follows on the Roman Catholic Church's teaching because its teachings about Mary are the most complete. We are aware that the Orthodox Church shares some of the developments found in the Catholic tradition. While it would be enjoyable to engage in a comparison of Catholic and Orthodox views of Mary, I would prefer that to be done by experts in those traditions.

In order to represent the Roman Catholic viewpoint, we will quote Roman Catholic sources for official understandings of the areas we explore. It is important for all of us to learn to be fair in our descriptions of what others believe. Once again, Roman Catholics know that what they believe about Mary is a development of the New Testament, and that these beliefs are not necessarily found in explicit statements in the Bible. There is little reason, therefore, for me to state over and over that (1) such a view is not found in Scripture and (2) Roman Catholics accept this because of the role of sacred Tradition in the formation of their faith and beliefs. Take this as a banner over each of the following discussions.

In this and the next chapter we will look at the terms that express the ongoing development of the life of Mary in Roman Catholic teaching.

Revelation 12

What happened to Mary after Acts 1:14? Did she disappear? According to some Bible scholars, and this view often surprises evangelical Christians, Mary does appear one more time in the New Testament . . . in the twelfth chapter of Revelation. Here's the text, and I have italicized the expressions that lead some theologians to think Mary is the woman of Revelation 12. Because I've seen the surprise on some Protestants' faces when I've brought this to their attention, I suggest we look carefully at these verses from Revelation:

> A great and wondrous sign appeared in heaven: a woman clothed with the sun, with the moon under her feet and a crown of twelve stars on her head. *She was pregnant and cried out in pain as she was about to give birth.* Then another sign appeared in heaven: an enormous red dragon with seven heads and ten horns and seven crowns on its heads. Its tail swept a third of the stars out of the sky and flung them to the earth. *The dragon stood in front of the woman who was about to give birth, so that it might devour her child the moment he was born. She gave birth to a son, a male child, who "will rule all the nations with an iron scepter." And her child was snatched up to God and to his throne.* The woman fled into the wilderness to a place prepared for her by God, where she might be taken care of for 1,260 days.
>
> And there was war in heaven. Michael and his angels fought against the dragon, and the dragon and his angels fought back. . . .

When the dragon saw that he had been hurled to the earth, he pursued *the woman who had given birth to the male child*. The woman was given the two wings of a great eagle, so that she might fly to the place prepared for her in the wilderness, where she would be taken care of for a time, times and half a time, out of the serpent's reach. Then from his mouth the serpent spewed water like a river, to overtake the woman and sweep her away with the torrent. But the earth helped the woman by opening its mouth and swallowing the river that the dragon had spewed out of his mouth. Then the dragon was enraged at the woman and went off to make war against *the rest of her offspring—those who keep God's commands and hold fast their testimony about Jesus.*

Clearly, the woman of this vision in the Apocalypse gives birth to Jesus; that has to be Mary. Or, does it? What follows that birth of Jesus does not sound like Mary. So far as we know, Mary was not attacked by Satan as soon as she gave birth; Mary did not flee into the wilderness for 1,260 days (that we know)—though she did flee to Egypt; Mary's escape—the image of having wings—is not known to us; we know of nothing that suggests that the earth somehow protected Mary; we are not aware of anything in the New Testament—unless it be John's becoming her "son"—that suggests all the followers of Jesus are her "offspring." If the verse about the birth does sound like Mary, nothing else in the text does.

Protestants often counter the claim that Mary is the woman of Revelation 12 by observing that such an interpretation does not appear until the sixth century, that the author does not identify the woman as Mary, and that the details of the birth do not match the details of what happened at Bethlehem. There is a consensus among Protestant scholars that the "woman" of Revelation 12 symbolizes the People of God, Israel and the Church. Is it possible that this woman is *both Mary* and *the People of God*, or perhaps even Mary *and* Israel *and* the Church? Ben Witherington III, a notable evangelical scholar, believes so. Maybe more Protestants need to do careful and prayerful study of this passage.

Now let's look at a few terms that were used of Mary in the early churches—say in the first four or five centuries after Christ.

Sinless

The Roman Catholic Church believes and teaches that Mary was sinless. Here is a full statement from *The Catholic Encyclopedia*, and it reads like an encyclopedia (so give it a chance):

> Scripture and tradition agree in ascribing to Mary the greatest personal sanctity: She is conceived without the stain of original sin; she shows the greatest humility and patience in her daily life (Luke 1:38, 48); she exhibits an heroic patience under the most trying circumstances (Luke 2:7, 35, 48; John 19:25–27). When there is question of sin, Mary must always be excepted. . . . Theologians assert that Mary was impeccable, not by the essential perfection of her nature, but by a special Divine privilege. Moreover, the Fathers, at least since the fifth century, almost unanimously maintain that the Blessed Virgin never experienced the motions of concupiscence.

Here's the major statement from the *Catechism of the Catholic Church*:

Mary benefited first of all and uniquely from Christ's victory over sin: she was preserved from all stain of original sin and by a special grace of God committed no sin of any kind during her whole earthly life.

Official Catholic teaching does not believe Mary was born perfectly mature, but instead that Mary grew in her faith and developed morally. Still, the official teaching is that in the process of maturation she did not sin. Yes, she was faced with temptations, but no, she didn't succumb to temptations. Yes, she could have sinned, but no, she didn't sin.

This must be said about what Catholics believe: Mary's sinlessness was not because she was divine. Mary's sinlessness in official teaching is solely the product of God's grace. The Greek word *kecharitomene* in Luke 1:28 is translated "you are highly favored" in *Today's New International Version*. But, in Roman Catholic theology that word is often translated "full of grace," which is a fair and literal rendering. This leads to the Catholic conclusion that she who is *full* of grace cannot and did not sin. The important point is that Mary's sinlessness is understood in Catholic theology as God's gracious work, not Mary's meritorious work.

Clearly, Roman Catholics know that not all Christians have agreed with the idea that Mary was sinless. *The Catholic Encyclopedia* prefaces the paragraph quoted above by a brief sketch of some early Christian theologians who believed that Mary sinned. The only appropriate response to this teaching is for each person to examine what the Bible says, what the Church has said, and then arrive at a conclusion. In particular, the evangelical will want to examine three passages in the Gospels: Jesus' surprising choice to remain at the Temple when he was twelve and Mary's words to him, Mary's words to Jesus at Cana, and then Mary's attempt to get Jesus to return to Nazareth early in his ministry, texts already discussed in this book.

It may come as a surprise to many readers to know that St. Augustine, who famously argued for the teaching of the utter sinfulness of everyone, and who shaped both the Catholic and the Protestant Church's understanding of original sin, himself believed that Mary was sinless. Here are his words, which often startle Protestants:

> We must *except the holy Virgin Mary*, concerning whom *I wish to raise no question* when it touches the subject of sins, out of honor to the Lord; for from Him we know *what abundance of grace for overcoming sin in every particular was conferred upon her* who had the merit to conceive and bear Him who undoubtedly had no sin.

Augustine was followed by many in this conclusion, including some major Protestant theologians—such as Martin Luther.

Yet, prior to Augustine many believed that Mary sinned and needed personal redemption. As Tim Perry summarizes this period of church history, "For the church fathers from Ignatius to Athanasius, Mary was a human being who erred by demonstrating impatience, lack of faith and doubt." On these points, many of us today would agree.

If one unfolds Mary's sinlessness in Catholic theology, one also discovers two other dimensions of what Catholics believe about Mary. She is the *Second Eve* and she is the *Mother of the Church*. If Jesus was predicted in the Old Testament, why not Mary? No one disputes that Isaiah's seventh chapter predicted that Jesus would be born of a virgin, but are there are other passages that anticipate Mary?

This is precisely the question Irenaeus, a great defender of the apostolic faith, asked about one hundred years after Jesus. "The knot of Eve's disobedience was untied by Mary's obedience," he said. One Old Testament verse that gave rise to the view that Mary was the Second Eve can be found at Genesis 3:15:

> And I will put enmity
> > between you and the woman,
> > and between your offspring and hers;
> he will crush your head,
> > and you will strike his heel.

In essence, the argument is this: As Eve disobeyed, so Mary obeyed. As Eve's sin led to the unmaking of others, so Mary's choice not to sin led to the remaking of others. Accordingly, as Adam disobeyed, so Jesus obeyed. Thus: if there is a Second Adam (Christ), there is also a Second Eve (Mary). Again, for some evangelicals this is tantamount to blasphemy, for it virtually places Mary alongside Jesus in the redemptive work of God. However grating such an idea might be, the analogy was made within a century of Jesus, and it has shaped Roman Catholic theology.

Mother of God

Roman Catholics have never hesitated to call Mary the "mother of God." The expression gives evangelicals alarm. Should it? If Jesus is God and Mary is his mother, then Mary is the mother of God. Please note, "mother of God" does not mean the one who existed before God and gave birth to God, but the one who "carried" God in her womb as the "God-bearer." It is reasonable to connect Jesus to God, Mary to Jesus and Mary as mother of God, but the Protestant impulse is *sola scriptura*: "to the Bible we go first."

Does the New Testament teach that Mary is the "mother of God"? Elizabeth asked this of Mary: "But why am I so favored, that the *mother of my* Lord should come to me?" Mother of God, Mother of the Lord—is there a difference? For most of us, it is far easier to speak of Mary as the "mother of the Lord" than to speak of her as the "mother of God." Still, we have to admit there is some biblical support for calling Mary "mother of God" or "mother of the Lord."

What we can agree on is that the expression "mother of God" played a very significant role in one of the major clashes in the development of our orthodox Christian understanding of Jesus Christ, the Second Person of the Trinity. In AD 431, the Council of Ephesus addressed the teachings of Nestorius, who maintained that Mary gave birth to a man named Jesus but that she did not give birth to the Word. In effect, Nestorius divided Jesus into a God part and a human part. The Council of Ephesus disagreed and settled for a major, major conclusion: Jesus' deity and humanity, his two natures, were *perfectly fused into one person*, so that Jesus was not both God *and* man but the God-man. If Jesus is the God-man of one person and not just God *and* man, then Mary gave birth to the single person who is the God-Man. If she did, then Mary was in some sense the "God-bearer" and not simply the "Christ-bearer" (as Nestorius taught).

Here's an important observation: The expression "God-bearer" soon shifted into the expression "mother of God." So, when theologians speak of "mother of God" they mean "God-bearer." We Protestants can, and rightfully should, stand with the whole Church on the importance of what the Council of Ephesus decided. If "Mother of God" means "God-bearer" as the one who gave birth to the human Jesus who, as a single person was the God-man, then we can also stand together with Roman Catholics in affirming Mary as the "Mother of God."

For many of us neither "God-bearer" nor "Mother of God" is the issue. The question we ask is this: Does addressing Mary as "Mother of God" involve veneration, adoration, and devotion of Mary as well? Does it get mixed up with "Wife of God" or even "Mother of the Trinity"? Does it result in giving attention to Mary or does it, as it originally was intended to do, give attention to Jesus Christ as fully God and fully human as the God-man? Because of the implications of what "mother of God" might mean, most Protestants shy away from calling Mary the "mother of God," but we should have no hesitation in referring to Mary as the "God-bearer."

Perpetually virgin

The Gospel of Matthew, in the first chapter, tells us that Joseph "had no union with her until she gave birth to a son." What most of us evangelicals believe is that *after* Mary gave birth to Jesus, Joseph *did* have union with Mary. What surprises Protestants is that Catholics (and the Orthodox) don't think Joseph and Mary had that union—ever. This never-having-union is called the perpetual virginity of Mary.

The belief that Mary was perpetually virgin developed early in the Church. It's important to note that such a belief about Mary arose alongside a commitment to celibacy as the noblest form of the spiritual life. Origen, who was the first major theologian of the Church (early third century) and who was also celibate, said this in his commentary on John: "There is no child of Mary except Jesus, *according to the opinion of those who think correctly about her.*" And he also said she "did not know any relations with a man" and "with regard to purity which consists in chastity, Jesus was the first among men, while Mary was the first among women."

A little more than a century later, Jerome (345–419) wrote a scathing attack on a contemporary Roman theologian named Helvidius who believed exactly what the majority of Protestants believe today: Joseph and Mary had sexual relations, and they had children from such unions. The most famous case made by Jerome was that "brothers and sisters" in the Gospel record could mean "cousins" or "relatives." This view has been maintained throughout the history of the Roman Catholic Church. Jerome, too, was deeply committed to celibacy and thought marriage was, if we read him generously, good but also a much more demanding lifestyle for spiritual formation. In other words, for Jerome celibacy was the higher form of spirituality.

From the time of Jerome on, most Christians affirmed that Mary never had sexual relations with Joseph. The issues were essentially one of demonstrating that what some thought the Bible stated may in fact not be what the Bible stated. Here we need to remind ourselves what was said in chapter eleven: first, that the statement "until she gave birth," from Matthew 1, might not have meant that afterwards Mary and Joseph had sexual relations; and second, that "brothers" can mean stepbrothers or cousins. If one accepts this interpretation of Scripture, then the widespread belief in the perpetual virginity is possible.

What perpetual virginity teaches about Mary is that her task was so holy and that her womb was so sanctified by the grace of God that Joseph concluded, out of reverence for what God had done, that he simply would not "invade" what was holy. Though we may not agree that Joseph considered such thoughts, we can understand why some conclude that Mary was perpetually virgin.

These three beliefs about Mary—that she was sinless, that she was the "mother of God," and that she was perpetually virgin— developed very early in the Church. We now will turn to some later developments in the Catholic Church.

13

Protestants, Roman Catholics, and Mary

WOMAN OF CONTROVERSY 2: *The Later Developments*

Julian Charley, a British theologian, brings to the surface the instinct of Protestants when he says this of the developments in Roman Catholic beliefs about Mary: "the overall impression [of what Catholicism teaches about Mary] is a picture that bears little resemblance to what we find in the New Testament. . . . Mary is extolled to a height that conveys almost semi-divine status, despite all the protestations [by Catholics] to the contrary." Because the terms we now need to discuss are so volatile to some Protestants and correspondingly precious to some Roman Catholics, let's be especially careful to understand them clearly and correctly.

Immaculate conception

Roman Catholics use two terms that lay Protestants regularly confuse: *virginal* conception and *immaculate* conception. The first refers to the supernatural conception of Jesus in the womb of Mary who was herself a virgin at the time of the conception. The second expression, immaculate conception, refers to the *supernatural preservation* of Mary from sin from the moment of her conception in her mother's womb. Mary was herself conceived normally; her mother and father had sexual relations, producing a baby. But, the instant Mary was conceived, so the teaching about the immaculate conception contends, God graciously worked in her so that she would be "immaculate," or without sin.

It was not until 1854 that Mary's immaculate conception became official Catholic teaching. Pope Pius IX, on the eighth of December, declared it official that Mary was immaculately conceived. Notice the words in italics and then the consequences of not believing the dogma:

> We declare, pronounce, and define that the doctrine which holds that the most Blessed Virgin Mary, in the first instance of her conception, by a singular grace and privilege granted by Almighty God, in view of the merits of Jesus Christ, the Savior of the human race, was preserved free from all stain of original sin, is a doctrine revealed by God and therefore to be believed firmly and constantly by all the faithful.
>
> Hence, if anyone shall dare—which God forbid!—to think otherwise than as has been defined by us, let him

know and understand that he is condemned by his own judgment; that he has suffered shipwreck in the faith; that he has separated from the unity of the Church; and that, furthermore, by his own action he incurs the penalties established by law if he should dare to express in words or writing or by any other outward means the errors he thinks in his heart.

We Protestants instinctually sympathize to some degree with this doctrine because we believe in original sin—that each of us is born as a little sinner. I have heard Protestant theologians state that original sin is the most demonstrable thing we believe: Just read the newspaper. The correlation between humans born and humans who sin is so high (it hovers right at a one-to-one ratio!) that one must conclude humans are born that way.

Not only have we learned about original sin, but most of us have also learned that the *virginal* conception (of Jesus) occurred in order to preserve Jesus from original sin. Our belief raises this question: If Jesus was preserved from original sin by not having a father, did Mary have original sin that she could pass on to Jesus? If one believes that all are born in sin, then Mary was also born with a sinful nature. If that is the case (and I can't deny it), then did she pass on her sinful nature to Jesus? If we say "no," we have to explain it. Enter the doctrine of the immaculate conception. The immaculate conception is the belief that Mary was by God's gracious work cleansed so she would not pass on a sinful nature to her son. Whether we agree with this dogma or not, it makes clear sense to Protestants.

Still, I wish to make one observation that has become a settled conviction on my part after years of thinking about what the Gospels say about the virginal conception and what they don't say. The New Testament *never* connects Jesus' "sinlessness" to the virginal conception. The connection between Jesus' sinlessness and the virginal conception is connection made by *Christian theologians*, but the writers of the New Testament didn't make that connection. And this leads me to these questions: If God can by a sheer act of grace and purity transform Mary in her mother's womb into a sinless creature, why could we not believe that God would simply have performed a miracle with Jesus in the womb of Mary? Or, is the immaculate conception necessary? Protestants might well argue that the immaculate conception makes sense or that it is consistent with Jesus' sinlessness, but they also want to ask this: Is it biblical and is it necessary?

Glorious assumption

Because Roman Catholics believe Mary was immaculately conceived and sinless, and because sin's consequences are disease, aging, and death, they also concluded that Mary's end could have been, and indeed was, abnormal. Instead of dying and decaying as other humans, Mary "died" in the presence of others, yet when they checked on her tomb she was gone. This is called the "glorious assumption" of Mary, and the event is celebrated by Roman Catholics on August 15. John of Damascus, the highly esteemed seventh-century theologian, pulled together various traditions about Mary's death and stated it like this:

St. Juvenal, Bishop of Jerusalem, at the Council of Chalcedon (451), made known to the Emperor Marcian and Pulcheria, who wished to possess the body of the Mother of God, that Mary died in the presence of all the Apostles, but that her tomb, when opened, upon the request of St. Thomas, was found empty; wherefrom the Apostles concluded that the body was taken up to heaven.

This conviction became official dogma on the first of November, 1950, when Pope Pius XII declared it binding and infallible dogma:

By the authority of our Lord Jesus Christ, of the Blessed Apostles Peter and Paul, and by our own authority, we pronounce, declare, and define it to be a divinely revealed dogma: that the Immaculate Mother of God, the ever Virgin Mary, having completed the course of her earthly life, was assumed body and soul into heavenly glory.

There is, of course, biblical warrant for humans being "assumed" into heaven: In the fifth chapter of Genesis, we read these words: "Enoch walked faithfully with God; then he was no more, because God took him away." About Elijah, the great prophet, the second chapter in 2 Kings says this: "When the LORD was about to take Elijah up to heaven in a whirlwind. . . ." Then later, after Elijah blessed his successor Elisha, the Bible records this:

As they were walking along and talking together, suddenly a chariot of fire and horses of fire appeared and separated the two of them, and Elijah went up to heaven in a whirlwind. Elisha saw this and cried out, "My father! My father! The chariots and horsemen of Israel!" And Elisha saw him no more. Then he took hold of his garment and tore it in two.

And, of Jesus, the first chapter of Acts records a similar event: "After he said this, he was taken up before their very eyes, and a cloud hid him from their sight." Such things can happen.

The question we need to ask about Mary is this: Was she also taken into the presence of God miraculously? As Protestants we go to the Bible first, but we find nothing about Mary's death or her assumption in the Bible. Does that mean Mary wasn't "assumed" into heaven? Obviously not. None of us believes that everything was recorded in the Bible, so we are left to examine the evidence and make up our own minds.

The Mediatrix

I have heard more than one Roman Catholic student say that he or she "prays to Mary." One student even told me he prayed to Mary because, as he put it, "she takes care of stuff for me with her Son." Many of us are justifiably worried by such comments, but it is a classic example of Protestants not hearing what is meant by such statements as well as an example of Roman Catholics not saying precisely what Roman Catholic teaching declares. Simply put, we Protestants need to learn that in official teaching, Roman Catholics pray *to Mary* by asking her to *intercede for them*.

Roman Catholicism has for centuries taught that Mary was in some sense the *Mediatrix*, the female mediator between sinful humans and an all-holy Son. In so teaching, however, Roman Catholics have never argued that Mary was divine or that the Trinity really was a Quadrinity (Father, Son, Mother, Spirit). And they do not believe the Son of God can be manipulated by his mother. Roman Catholics have always maintained that Jesus Christ is the only Mediator between God and humans, and that the apostle Paul made this clear when he said in the second chapter of his first letter to Timothy that there is "one God and one mediator between God and human beings, Christ Jesus, himself human."

So how can Roman Catholics arrive at the idea that Mary is a Mediatrix? According to Catholic teachings, the notion unfolds from the fact that Paul, in the third chapter of his first letter to the churches at Corinth, said that he and others were "God's co-workers." Scott Hahn, a Roman Catholic theologian, speaks of Mary's "co-working" with God in this way: "In short, the Father willed that His Son's entire existence as a man would hinge, so to speak, upon the ongoing consent of Mary." That is, God's redemptive work hinged upon Mary's being a co-worker with God when she said "may it be" or "do whatever he tells you."

The singular example of this in the Bible is Mary's going to Jesus at the wedding of Cana and asking her son to provide wine. Even though Jesus' words distance himself from his mother, in the end Jesus (son of Mary) did what his mother requested: He made wine for everyone. Mary, so it is taught, *interceded* with her son for others.

In short, Mary's so-called mediation is the mediation of a human between her divine Son and other humans just like her. Inevitably, this attracts attention to Mary to the degree that many of us think Roman Catholics have a tendency—or, as many see it, more than just a tendency—to elevate Mary so high that she becomes an idol. "Not so!" said Pope John Paul II in his influential book on Mary called *Mary: God's Yes to Man*. The wedding at Cana, he said, indeed "offers us *a sort of first announcement of*

Mary's mediation," but her mediation does not call attention to herself; instead, it is "wholly oriented toward Christ and tending to the revelation of his salvific power."

Not only does Mary's "mediation" point to Christ, the Vatican claims, but also her mediation is based one hundred percent on the saving power and mediation of Jesus Christ. At the Second Vatican Council a document was published called *Lumen Gentium*, "The Dogmatic Constitution on the Church," with a chapter called "Our Lady." In paragraph 60 of that statement we find this about Mary's "mediation":

> It flows forth from the superabundance of the merits of Christ, rests on his mediation, depends entirely on it and draws all its power from it. It does not hinder in any way the immediate union of the faithful with Christ but on the contrary fosters it.

If we are committed to being fair with one another, then, we have to admit that Roman Catholics do not teach in the mediation of Mary that she is anything more than a human being, nor do they teach that her mediation detracts from Christ.

This is according to official teaching. The issue, as is often also the case with Protestant thinking, is not just a case of official teaching. How the official teaching is appropriated and expressed by the laity often raises questions. When we see at multitudes of junctions in Italy a small picture, a shrine, or a small statue of *Maria e bambino* ("Mary and the baby"), we are led to think of Mary as the dominating figure and Jesus as the dependent figure. When we enter Roman Catholic cathedrals and basilicas and find pictures or statues of Mary over the altar and only on the back wall, in ways less accessible, pictures or statues of Jesus, we are led to think that Mary is more prominent than her son. Official teaching is otherwise; perception is something else.

Some Roman Catholics explain Mary's mediation as little more than what is often called "the communion of the saints." That is, all Christians—past, present, and future—are in a mystical communion now and forever with God and with one another. The saints who have gone before us are, it needs to be emphasized, alive in the presence of God. Mary is part of that communion. And so it is reasoned that if we can ask our friends or pastors or parents to pray for us, why can't we ask Mary to pray for us? For most of us Protestants the response is knee-jerk: There is no evidence in the Bible that God's people asked dead saints to pray for them so (we conclude) we shouldn't practice such prayers of intercession. Still, we might learn to ask ourselves this question: If we believe in the communion of saints and that the saints are in the presence of God, is it appropriate for us to ask them to pray for us?

In our attempts to be fair we also have to be honest. Our concern is similar with Mary's "mediation" as it is with any other of the traditional developments in the Catholic Church: Does such a practice elevate Mary too high so that she becomes the chief one to whom one goes for prayer? Could such ideas gradually encroach on the role and dignity of Jesus and lead some to believe that Mary is semi-divine? Which leads us directly to a final issue: devotion to Mary.

Devotion to Mary

Devotion to Mary is not essential to the Roman Catholic faith. It does, however, seem to be on the rise, and, as many of us took note, Pope John Paul II himself was ardently devoted to Mary. Once again, fairness requires us to do our best to understand what is taught.

First, let us begin with some terms. Different people use them differently, so for clarity let's define our terms and be consistent. In spite of what is sometimes repeated as urban legend, Roman Catholics *clearly* distinguish God—Father, Son, Spirit—from Mary. "Worship" and "adoration," it is taught, are only appropriate for God, but it is appropriate to "honor" and "venerate" Mary (and other saints). Epiphanius, a fourth-century bishop from near the Holy Land, laid down a rule: "Let Mary be held in *honor*. Let the Father, Son, and Holy Ghost be *adored*, but let no one *adore* Mary."

Second, much more so than most Protestants—even those who routinely recite the Apostles' Creed with its belief in the communion of saints, Roman Catholics have a lively belief in the living reality of all saints, especially martyrs and heroes of the faith. Devotion to Mary, therefore, has to do with *remembering* her, *expressing thanks to God* for her role in being the mother of the Messiah and for her exemplary character, routinely *commemorating* her birthday, annunciation, and dormition (her death and assumption), and a bold *veneration* of the sanctity of her role in God's work.

Third, some have claimed that Mary has appeared to them. Jon Sweeney, a Protestant who has made a careful study of Mary, wittily put it this way: "Mary sometimes seems like the attic ghost that will not rest." The stories of (supposed) appearances are well known about Medjugorje, Lourdes, Fatima, and Guadalupe. Whether or not one believes such appearances are genuine, we all will admit that at least the claims of appearances express a theology of devotion to Mary. Protestants are prone to point out that devotion to Mary *can* go too far. For some of this, the words of one Pope are clear evidence:

On February 2, 1849, Pope Pius IX, in his *Ubi Primum* encyclical, expressed this Marian devotion more graphically than anything I've seen:

> *From our earliest years nothing has ever been closer to Our heart than devotion—filial, profound, and wholehearted—to the most blessed Virgin Mary. Always have We endeavored to do everything that would redound to the greater glory of the Blessed Virgin, promote her honor, and encourage devotion to her. . . .*

> Great indeed is Our trust in Mary. The resplendent glory of her merits, far exceeding all the choirs of angels, elevates her to the very steps of the throne of God. Her foot has crushed the head of Satan. Set up between Christ and His Church, Mary, ever lovable and full of grace, always has delivered the Christian people from their greatest calamities and from the snares and assaults of all their enemies, ever rescuing them from ruin.

> And likewise in our own day, Mary, with the ever merciful affection so characteristic of her maternal heart, wishes, through her efficacious intercession with God, to deliver her children from the sad and grief-laden troubles, from the tribulations, the anxiety, the difficulties, and the punishments

of God's anger which afflict the world because of the sins of men. Wishing to restrain and to dispel the violent hurricane of evils which, as We lament from the bottom of Our heart, are everywhere afflicting the Church, Mary desires to transform Our sadness into joy. *The foundation of all Our confidence, as you know well, Venerable Brethren, is found in the Blessed Virgin Mary.* For, God has committed to Mary the treasury of all good things, in order that everyone may know that through her are obtained every hope, every grace, and all salvation. *For this is His will, that we obtain everything through Mary.*

Not all Roman Catholics would say what Pius IX said. Still, these words illustrate the lengths to which devotion to Mary can extend. We can't be surprised that alongside such devotion came official warnings about exaggeration. *Lumen Gentium*, the important statement from Vatican II, warned theologians and preachers: "let them rightly illustrate the duties and privileges of the Blessed Virgin which *always refer to Christ.*"

However, we can't blame devotion to Mary on some superstitious medieval age. Devotion to Mary began early, and I take as an example none other than the arch-orthodox defender and definer of how we all understand the doctrine of the Trinity, Athanasius. Here is something he wrote in his Homily of the Papyrus of Turin. "Oh noble virgin, truly you are greater than any other greatness. For who is your equal in greatness, O dwelling place of God the Word? To whom among all creatures shall I compare you, O Virgin? You are greater than them all. . . . If I say that heaven is exalted, yet it does not equal you. . . ."

Scanning these last two chapters, it would be fair to say that Mary has become an origami figure of unfolding developments in Roman Catholic theology. Each of the themes connected to Mary has a hint or a suggestion in the New Testament, and each, over time and at the hands of some of the most famous theologians of the Church, has undergone intense development, if also to extremes at times. In an age such as ours is today, when cooperation between Christians of all sizes and shapes will be required, we can begin today—and I speak to my evangelical community directly—to converse thoughtfully with one another if only we will take the time to understand what each segment of the Church believes.

Now that we have sketched the life of the real Mary and have surveyed how that life generated an ongoing development, we are ready to consider how we as Protestants can learn to embrace the real Mary in our own times.

part III
Embracing the Real Mary

14

"All generations will call me blessed"
WOMAN TO REMEMBER

In the Magnificat, Mary, in the power of the Spirit, predicted that "from now on all generations will call me blessed." Mary might have predicted that "from now on all generations—except Protestants—will call me blessed." Roman Catholics and the Eastern Orthodox have always "blessed" Mary. In fact, according to church calendars, Roman Catholics have at least 15 days a year dedicated to blessing Mary! Protestants, however, in our efforts ever since the Reformation to distance ourselves from Catholics, have failed to render Mary her due.

It is time for us to give the real Mary her due, to honor her for who she is. The real Mary was an ordinary Jewish woman with an extraordinary vocation who struggled, as all ordinary Jews did, with who Jesus was. Through her struggle, she came to terms with the difficult reality that the Messiah's mission—unlike Mary's expectations—was to die for others. This real Mary, the one who struggled to embrace Jesus' mission, is no offense to Protestants, but rather she is a woman for us to honor.

So, I'm calling for an event: a single day in each local Protestant church, and I suggest we call it "Honor Mary Day." And alongside such a day, I am asking for Christians to gather together in discussion to examine once again what the Bible actually says about the real Mary. If we do have an Honor Mary Day, what exactly will we celebrate? The story of Mary, the story of how the real Mary learned in her Jewish world that the Messianic dream would come about not through military triumph or through the use of might but through the paradoxical power of the Cross, the Resurrection, and the empowering presence of God's Holy Spirit. The real Mary's story is a story about a faith that struggles and learns and grows until it comes to terms with what God is doing in this world through the Son.

Perhaps we could begin by apologizing in the words of the Welsh Baptist poet and New Testament specialist John Gwili Jenkins:

> Forgive us, gentle maiden, if we learnt to give you
> Less respect than heaven would have wished;
> For we fell in love with the Son of your great love,
> So as not to venerate you more than Him.

After this apology of sorts, I suggest we focus on five themes in Mary's life. (Also see Appendix 2, Suggestions for Reflecting on Mary, which is chock full of Scripture references, prayers, and hymns to enhance any Honor Mary Day.)

Faith leads us to Jesus

John the Baptist, it has been said, had one mission: to point to Jesus. It was no different for Mary: She, too, pointed to Jesus. Her song, the Magnificat, pointed to Jesus because it extolled what God would do through the Messiah. Mary was not perfect, but even when Mary botched a situation her failures somehow pointed toward Jesus. And when we observe the grieving Mary at the cross, she was focused on her son. The real Mary pointed to Jesus.

In particular, Mary leads us to a Jesus who brings redemption, not by the power of the sword, not by the display of might, and not by the storming of Jerusalem, but by the difficult and counter-intuitive power of forgiveness created by self-sacrificing love. To listen to Mary is to hear the message of Jesus' death and resurrection as a mega-event whereby God established a new kind of power, a new kind of family, and a new kind of kingdom.

The Anglican poet G.A. Studdert Kennedy puts together Mary's witness to Jesus remarkably well:

> She claims no crown from Christ apart,
> Who gave God life and limb,
> She only claims a broken heart,
> Because of him.

Faith is uniquely personal

Permit me to make a distinction between two terms: "model" and "example." People often use these terms interchangeably, but "model" describes something we imitate and "example" defines a specific behavior. To make Mary a "model," as if she were the ideal type, can be harmful. Only Jesus is the ideal for the Christian. Mary is not a model, for no one else can be both virginal and a mother! No one else can be the mother of the Messiah. No one else can sing the Magnificat as she did.

We run a serious risk making anyone a model because everyone's life—yours, Mary's and mine—is uniquely personal. As Nancy Duff, professor of Christian ethics at Princeton, puts it, "God does not encounter Mary or any of us as ideals, nor does God transform us into ideals. We are like Mary, real human beings of flesh and spirit, body and soul, in need of the power of God as we seek to give glory to the One who saves and sustains us in grace. Mary, like all of us, was called not into perfection but into discipleship. . . . We are called in this world to real tasks, not ideal ones."

But Mary can serve us well as an "example" of learning to follow Jesus in the real world. Mary's life was uniquely personal. She was a young Jewish woman; she was poor; she was engaged; and God chose for her to conceive virginally. The challenge for her to trust God in that situation was uniquely hers. Her battles were hers, unlike anything we will ever face. She trusted God in her world, in her way, for her times, and she was challenged (as we are) to accomplish God's plan for her (or our) particular life.

What we can learn from Mary's example is to ask not "How can I be like Mary?" but instead "What can I learn from Mary about living in faith in my real world?" You and I have to learn how to live our own lives, in our own families, in our own world, in our own vocations, etc. Mary isn't a model we are called to imitate, but an example of a real person trusting God as an individual.

There is a real danger in making Mary a super-saint. If we make too much of Mary, she becomes not "chosen by God" but "god-like." She becomes not an ordinary Jewish woman with an extraordinary vocation and ordinary faith, but a super-ordinary Jewish woman with a super-ordinary vocation with super-ordinary faith. When the latter happens, she becomes a goddess. *The Real Mary* has labored to show that she was neither a goddess nor a super-saint. She was special, I agree, but she was special because she trusted God as an ordinary woman with an extraordinary vocation with ordinary faith. She was special because she struggled through the realities of learning what kind of Messiah her son would be.

Faith is real

Mary's faith was real. An "Honor Mary Day" would emphasize the real faith of real people. It is easy to fall prey to romanticizing Mary's faith and turning her into a saint wearing a powder blue robe. She was a real human (like us) with a real faith (like ours) in the real world (like ours).

And our faith is faith only if it too is real. We don't walk six inches off the ground any more than Mary did. Each of us knows the challenge to trust God can overwhelm our capacities, sometimes the way of the cross confronts our own expectations, and sometimes centering our life in the family of God cuts into the grain of what we'd rather do. Perhaps we'd rather leverage our power than kneel before the Son of God who established a new kind of kingdom with a new kind of power.

Real faith is about trusting God to get through my struggles today in my real world. It is found in moms and dads, brothers and sisters, children and parents, bosses and employees, the employed and the unemployed, the fortunate and the tragic in the church and outside the church.

Faith develops

Faith develops. No one wakes up on Day Two of discipleship with perfect faith. Sometimes we trust and sometimes we don't. By setting aside an "Honor Mary Day," we will find Mary to be an example of someone who tells the story of the need for our faith to develop and grow daily.

Conversion is a life-long process of being transformed. Some of us think the apostle Paul's dramatic conversion experience on the Damascus Road is the norm, but it is far more likely that the story of the real Mary is the norm. Mary's faith developed: She was smitten with the dynastic notion that God was about to make her son the king of Israel. But she soon learned, as she watched and learned to follow her own son as the Messiah, that such an idea of an earthly Davidic dynasty set up in Jerusalem gave way to the formation of something else, namely a faith family, that would branch out into the whole world. She wrestled with her son, even opposing the work he did. It is true, as the evangelical scholar Tim Perry says, that Mary's life "is one that mirrors the lives of many believers, with moments of intense spirituality interrupted by extended periods of ambiguity."

As we think of our faith on a day we honor Mary, we might also celebrate the faith family that Mary herself—and we—grew into. Not only is faith something between the individual and God, but also it is something that we share with others—

something we share with Mary—something Mary shared with that circle of followers who sat at Jesus' feet to learn how to do God's will.

Faith is courageous and dangerous

Finally, as we honor Mary, we could celebrate the danger of a courageous faith. Perhaps on such a day we could imagine what God might do through us if we had the courageous faith that Mary had. The lesson of the Magnificat is the lesson of a woman willing to declare that God will bring justice in the teeth of oppression.

No one finds challenges easy. Sometimes we are granted a vision that could change our church or our neighborhood or our community, and usually we do not feel "capable" or "called." Faith in such visions will require courage. It may be dangerous to our community for us to catch the wave of this kind of vision. We will need courageous faith.

Mary's challenge came from God—to give birth to the Messiah of Israel. Mary knew what that meant to Herod the Great and to Caesar Augustus. She was challenged to conceive as a virgin, and she realized the cost to her reputation, to her husband, and to her son. But she trusted God. Trusting God took courage. Her singular act of faith turned the key that opened the world to the birth of the Messiah, and the world has never been the same.

Not only did Mary have courage in her convictions, but also she had *chutzpah*, the confidence that she knew what God was doing in the world. Mary knew who Jesus was called to be, what he was called to do, and she knew what God said Jesus would accomplish as Messiah, and *what she knew gave her the confidence* at times to *disagree with Jesus*. You and I may stand aghast at her confrontations with Jesus now, but at the same time we have to admire the strength of Mary's faith: She may have been wrong, but she was wrong because she was confident in what she believed God was about to do.

As Kathleen Norris has said so well in her own reflections about Mary, "When I am called to answer 'Yes' to God, not knowing where this commitment will lead me, Mary gives me hope that it is enough to trust in God's grace and promise of salvation."

Perhaps on a day dedicated to honoring Mary we could be empowered to dream the Magnificat dream for our society. Perhaps we could be encouraged to let our hearts and minds swell with bigger thoughts for our world. People of courageous faith change the world.

Appendix 1

Old Testament Parallels in
The Magnificat

Luke 1:46b-47: *My soul glorifies the* LORD *and my spirit rejoices in God my Savior,*

Ps. 34:3: Glorify the LORD with me; let us exalt his name together.

Ps. 35:9: Then my soul will rejoice in the LORD and delight in his salvation.

Isa. 61:10: I delight greatly in the LORD; my soul rejoices in my God. For he has clothed me with garments of salvation and arrayed me in a robe of his righteousness, as a bridegroom adorns his head like a priest, and as a bride adorns herself with her jewels.

1 Sam. 2:1–2: Then Hannah prayed and said: "My heart rejoices in the lord; in the LORD my horn is lifted high. My mouth boasts over my enemies, for I delight in your deliverance. "There is no one holy like the LORD; there is no one besides you; there is no Rock like our God.

Hab. 3:18: yet I will rejoice in the LORD; I will be joyful in God my Savior.

Luke 1:48a: *for he has been mindful of the humble state of his servant.*

1 Sam. 1:11: And she [Hannah] made a vow, saying, "LORD Almighty, if you will only look on your servant's misery and remember me, and not forget your servant but give her a son, then I will give him to the LORD for all the days of his life, and no razor will ever be used on his head."

1 Sam. 9:16: "About this time tomorrow I will send you a man from the land of Benjamin. Anoint him ruler over my people Israel; he will deliver them from the hand of the Philistines. I have looked on my people, for their cry has reached me."

Gen. 29:32: Leah became pregnant and gave birth to a son. She named him Reuben, for she said, "It is because the LORD has seen my misery. Surely my husband will love me now."

Luke 1:48b: *From now on all generations will call me blessed,*

Gen. 30:13: Then Leah said, "How happy I am! The women will call me happy." So she named him Asher.

Mal. 3:12: "Then all nations will call you blessed, for yours will be a delightful land," says the lord Almighty.

Luke 1:49a: *for the Mighty One has done great things for me—*

Deut. 10:21: He is your praise; he is your God, who performed for you those great and awesome wonders you saw with your own eyes.

Ps. 71:19b: You who have done great things. Who is like you, God?

Zeph. 3:17: The LORD your God is with you, the Mighty Warrior who saves. He will take great delight in you; in his love he will no longer rebuke you, but will rejoice over you with singing.

Luke 1:49b: *holy is his name.*

Ps. 111:9: He provided redemption for his people; he ordained his covenant forever—holy and awesome is his name.

Luke 1:50: *His mercy extends to those who fear him, from generation to generation.*

Ps. 103:11: For as high as the heavens are above the earth, so great is his love for those who fear him.

Ps. 103:17: But from everlasting to everlasting the LORD'S steadfast love is with those who fear him, and his righteousness with their children's children.

Ps. 100:5: For the LORD is good and his love endures forever; his faithfulness continues through all generations.

Luke 1:51–53: *He has shown mighty deeds with his arm; he has scattered those who are proud in their inmost thoughts. He has brought down rulers from their thrones but has lifted up the humble. He has filled the hungry with good things but has sent the rich away empty.*

1 Sam. 2:7-8: The LORD sends poverty and wealth; he humbles and he exalts. He raises the poor from the dust and lifts the needy from the ash heap; he seats them with princes and has them inherit a throne of honor. For the foundations of the earth are the LORD's, on them he has set the world.

Ps. 89:10: You crushed Rahab like one of the slain; with your strong arm you scattered your enemies.

Prov. 3:34: He mocks proud mockers but shows favor to the humble and oppressed.

Job 12:19: He leads priests away stripped and overthrows officials long established.

Ezek. 21:26b: The lowly will be exalted and the exalted will be brought low.

Ps. 107:9: For he satisfies the thirsty and fills the hungry with good things.

Luke 1:54-55: *He has helped his servant Israel, remembering to be merciful to Abraham and to his descendants forever just as he promised our ancestors.*

Isa. 41:8-9: But you, Israel, my servant, Jacob, whom I have chosen, you descendants of Abraham, my friend, I took you from the ends of the earth, from its farthest corners I called you. I said, "You are my servant"; I have chosen you and have not rejected you.

Ps. 98:3: He has remembered his love and his faithfulness to the house of Israel; all the ends of the earth have seen the salvation of our God.

Mic. 7:20: You will be faithful to Jacob and show love to Abraham, as you pledged on oath to our ancestors in days long ago.

2 Sam. 22:51: He gives his king great victories; he shows unfailing kindness to his anointed, to David and his descendants forever.

Appendix 2:
Suggestions for *Reflecting on Mary*

SCRIPTURE REFLECTIONS

Ponder one or more of the following New Testament texts from *Today's New International Version*. Here are some good questions to ask:

What does the passage say about Mary?
How does the passage express Mary's faith in God?
What is Mary's relationship to Jesus in this passage?
How are Mary's relationships with others described?
What can you learn about real faith because of Mary?

The Gospel of Matthew

Matthew 1:18 This is how the birth of Jesus the Messiah came about: His mother Mary was pledged to be married to Joseph, but before they came together, she was found to be pregnant through the Holy Spirit. [19]Because Joseph her husband was a righteous man and did not want to expose her to public disgrace, he had in mind to divorce her quietly. [20]But after he had considered this, an angel of the Lord appeared to him in a dream and said, "Joseph son of David, do not be afraid to take Mary home as your wife, because what is conceived in her is from the Holy Spirit. [21]She will give birth to a son, and you are to give him the name Jesus, because he will save his people from their sins."

[22]All this took place to fulfill what the Lord had said through the prophet: [23] "The virgin will conceive and give birth to a son, and they will call him Immanuel" (which means "God with us"). [24]When Joseph woke up, he did what the angel of the Lord had commanded him and took Mary home as his wife. [25]But he had no union with her until she gave birth to a son. And he gave him the name Jesus.

The Gospel of Mark

Mark 3:31 Then Jesus' mother and brothers arrived. Standing outside, they sent someone in to call him. [32]A crowd was sitting around him, and they told him, "Your mother and brothers are outside looking for you."

[33]"Who are my mother and my brothers?" he asked.

^{34}Then he looked at those seated in a circle around him and said, "Here are my mother and my brothers! ^{35}Whoever does God's will is my brother and sister and mother."

Mark 6:1 Jesus left there and went to his hometown, accompanied by his disciples. ^{2}When the Sabbath came, he began to teach in the synagogue, and many who heard him were amazed.

"Where did this man get these things?" they asked. "What's this wisdom that has been given him? What are these remarkable miracles he is performing? ^{3}Isn't this the carpenter? Isn't this Mary's son and the brother of James, Joseph, Judas and Simon? Aren't his sisters here with us?" And they took offense at him.

^{4} Jesus said to them, "Only in their own towns, among their relatives and in their own homes are prophets without honor." ^{5}He could not do any miracles there, except lay his hands on a few sick people and heal them. ^{6}He was amazed at their lack of faith.

Then Jesus went around teaching from village to village.

Mark 15:40 Some women were watching from a distance. Among them were Mary Magdalene, Mary the mother of James the younger and of Joseph, and Salome. ^{41}In Galilee these women had followed him and cared for his needs. Many other women who had come up with him to Jerusalem were also there.

The Gospel of Luke

The Annunciation

Luke 1:26 In the sixth month of Elizabeth's pregnancy, God sent the angel Gabriel to Nazareth, a town in Galilee, [27]to a virgin pledged to be married to a man named Joseph, a descendant of David. The virgin's name was Mary. [28]The angel went to her and said, "Greetings, you who are highly favored! The Lord is with you."

[29]Mary was greatly troubled at his words and wondered what kind of greeting this might be. [30]But the angel said to her, "Do not be afraid, Mary, you have found favor with God. [31]You will conceive and give birth to a son, and you are to call him Jesus. [32]He will be great and will be called the Son of the Most High. The Lord God will give him the throne of his father David, [33]and he will reign over the house of Jacob forever; his kingdom will never end."

[34]"How will this be," Mary asked the angel, "since I am a virgin?"

[35]The angel answered, "The Holy Spirit will come on you, and the power of the Most High will overshadow you. So the holy one to be born will be called the Son of God. [36]Even Elizabeth your relative is going to have a child in her old age, and she who was said to be unable to conceive is in her sixth month. [37]For no word from God will ever fail."

[38]"I am the Lord's servant," Mary answered. "May it be to me according to your word." Then the angel left her.

The Magnificat

39At that time Mary got ready and hurried to a town in the hill country of Judea, 40where she entered Zechariah's home and greeted Elizabeth. 41When Elizabeth heard Mary's greeting, the baby leaped in her womb, and Elizabeth was filled with the Holy Spirit. 42In a loud voice she exclaimed: "Blessed are you among women, and blessed is the child you will bear! 43But why am I so favored, that the mother of my Lord should come to me? 44As soon as the sound of your greeting reached my ears, the baby in my womb leaped for joy. 45Blessed is she who has believed that the Lord would fulfill his promises to her!"

46And Mary said: "My soul glorifies the Lord 47and my spirit rejoices in God my Savior, 48for he has been mindful of the humble state of his servant.
From now on all generations will call me blessed,

49for the Mighty One has done great things for me—
holy is his name.

50His mercy extends to those who fear him,
from generation to generation.

51He has performed mighty deeds with his arm;
he has scattered those who are proud in their inmost thoughts.

52He has brought down rulers from their thrones
but has lifted up the humble.

53He has filled the hungry with good things
but has sent the rich away empty.

54He has helped his servant Israel,
remembering to be merciful

55to Abraham and his descendants forever,
just as he promised our ancestors."

⁵⁶Mary stayed with Elizabeth for about three months and then returned home.

The Birth of Jesus

Luke 2:1 In those days Caesar Augustus issued a decree that a census should be taken of the entire Roman world. ²(This was the first census that took place while Quirinius was governor of Syria.) ³And everyone went to their own town to register.

⁴So Joseph also went up from the town of Nazareth in Galilee to Judea, to Bethlehem the town of David, because he belonged to the house and line of David. ⁵He went there to register with Mary, who was pledged to be married to him and was expecting a child. ⁶While they were there, the time came for the baby to be born, ⁷and she gave birth to her firstborn, a son. She wrapped him in cloths and placed him in a manger, because there was no guest room available for them.

Luke 2:8 And there were shepherds living out in the fields nearby, keeping watch over their flocks at night. ⁹An angel of the Lord appeared to them, and the glory of the Lord shone around them, and they were terrified. ¹⁰But the angel said to them, "Do not be afraid. I bring you good news of great joy that will be for all the people. ¹¹Today in the town of David a Savior has been born to you; he is the Messiah, the Lord. ¹²This will be a sign to you: You will find a baby wrapped in cloths and lying in a manger."

¹³Suddenly a great company of the heavenly host appeared with the angel, praising God and saying,

[14]"Glory to God in the highest heaven,
and on earth peace to those on whom his favor rests."

Luke 2:15 When the angels had left them and gone into heaven, the shepherds said to one another, "Let's go to Bethlehem and see this thing that has happened, which the Lord has told us about." [16]So they hurried off and found Mary and Joseph, and the baby, who was lying in the manger. [17]When they had seen him, they spread the word concerning what had been told them about this child, [18]and all who heard it were amazed at what the shepherds said to them. [19]But Mary treasured up all these things and pondered them in her heart. [20]The shepherds returned, glorifying and praising God for all the things they had heard and seen, which were just as they had been told.

The Dedication and Purification

Luke 2:21 On the eighth day, when it was time to circumcise the child, he was named Jesus, the name the angel had given him before he was conceived.

[22]When the time came for the purification rites required by the Law of Moses, Joseph and Mary took him to Jerusalem to present him to the Lord [23](as it is written in the Law of the Lord, "Every firstborn male is to be consecrated to the Lord"), [24]and to offer a sacrifice in keeping with what is said in the Law of the Lord: "a pair of doves or two young pigeons."

Luke 2:25 Now there was a man in Jerusalem called Simeon, who was righteous and devout. He was waiting for the consolation of Israel, and the Holy Spirit was on him. [26]It had been revealed to him by the Holy Spirit that he would not die before he had seen the Lord's Messiah. [27]Moved by the Spirit, he went into the temple courts. When the parents brought in the child Jesus to do for him what the custom of the Law required, [28]Simeon took him in his arms and praised God, saying:

[29]"Sovereign Lord, as you have promised,
you may now dismiss your servant in peace.
[30]For my eyes have seen your salvation,
[31]which you have prepared in the sight of all nations:
[32]a light for revelation to the Gentiles,
and the glory of your people Israel."

Luke 2:33 The child's father and mother marveled at what was said about him. [34]Then Simeon blessed them and said to Mary, his mother: "This child is destined to cause the falling and rising of many in Israel, and to be a sign that will be spoken against, [35]so that the thoughts of many hearts will be revealed. And a sword will pierce your own soul too."

Luke 2:36 There was also a prophet, Anna, the daughter of Phanuel, of the tribe of Asher. She was very old; she had lived with her husband seven years after her marriage, [37]and then had been a widow for eighty-four years. She never left the temple but worshiped night and day, fasting and praying. [38]Coming up to them at that very moment, she gave thanks to God and spoke about the child to all who were looking forward to the redemption of Jerusalem.

Luke 2:39 When Joseph and Mary had done everything required by the Law of the Lord, they returned to Galilee to their own town of Nazareth. ^{40}And the child grew and became strong; he was filled with wisdom, and the grace of God was on him.

Jesus in the Temple at Twelve

Luke 2:41 Every year Jesus' parents went to Jerusalem for the Festival of the Passover. ^{42}When he was twelve years old, they went up to the Festival, according to the custom. ^{43}After the Festival was over, while his parents were returning home, the boy Jesus stayed behind in Jerusalem, but they were unaware of it. ^{44}Thinking he was in their company, they traveled on for a day. Then they began looking for him among their relatives and friends. ^{45}When they did not find him, they went back to Jerusalem to look for him. ^{46}After three days they found him in the temple courts, sitting among the teachers, listening to them and asking them questions. ^{47}Everyone who heard him was amazed at his understanding and his answers. ^{48}When his parents saw him, they were astonished. His mother said to him, "Son, why have you treated us like this? Your father and I have been anxiously searching for you."

^{49}"Why were you searching for me?" he asked. "Didn't you know I had to be in my Father's house?" ^{50}But they did not understand what he was saying to them.

^{51}Then he went down to Nazareth with them and was obedient to them. But his mother treasured all these things in her heart. ^{52}And as Jesus grew up, he increased in wisdom and in favor with God and people.

Luke 11:27 As Jesus was saying these things, a woman in the crowd called out, "Blessed is the mother who gave you birth and nursed you." ²⁸He replied, "Blessed rather are those who hear the word of God and obey it."

The Gospel of John

John 2:1 On the third day a wedding took place at Cana in Galilee. Jesus' mother was there, ²and Jesus and his disciples had also been invited to the wedding. ³When the wine was gone, Jesus' mother said to him, "They have no more wine."

⁴"Woman, why do you involve me?" Jesus replied. "My hour has not yet come."

⁵His mother said to the servants, "Do whatever he tells you."

⁶Nearby stood six stone water jars, the kind used by the Jews for ceremonial washing, each holding from twenty to thirty gallons.

⁷Jesus said to the servants, "Fill the jars with water"; so they filled them to the brim.

⁸Then he told them, "Now draw some out and take it to the master of the banquet." They did so, ⁹and the master of the banquet tasted the water that had been turned into wine. He did not realize where it had come from, though the servants who had drawn the water knew. Then he called the bridegroom aside ¹⁰and said, "Everyone brings out the choice wine first and then the cheaper wine after the guests

have had too much to drink; but you have saved the best till now."

11What Jesus did here in Cana of Galilee was the first of the signs through which he revealed his glory; and his disciples put their faith in him.

12After this he went down to Capernaum with his mother and brothers and his disciples. There they stayed for a few days.

John 19:25 Near the cross of Jesus stood his mother, his mother's sister, Mary the wife of Clopas, and Mary Magdalene. 26When Jesus saw his mother there, and the disciple whom he loved standing nearby, he said to her, "Woman, here is your son," 27and to the disciple, "Here is your mother." From that time on, this disciple took her into his home.

The Acts of the Apostles

Acts 1:12 Then the apostles returned to Jerusalem from the hill called the Mount of Olives, a Sabbath day's walk from the city. 13When they arrived, they went upstairs to the room where they were staying. Those present were Peter, John, James and Andrew; Philip and Thomas, Bartholomew and Matthew; James son of Alphaeus and Simon the Zealot, and Judas son of James. 14They all joined together constantly in prayer, along with the women and Mary the mother of Jesus, and with his brothers.

The Apostle Paul

Gal. 4:4 But when the set time had fully come, God sent his Son, born of a woman, born under the law.

Prayers and Hymns
From *The Book of Common Prayer*

The Presentation February 2
Almighty and ever living God, we humbly pray that, as your only-begotten Son was this day presented in the temple, so we may be presented to you with pure and clean hearts by Jesus Christ our Lord; who lives and reigns with you and the Holy Spirit, one God, now and for ever. Amen.

The Annunciation March 25
Pour your grace into our hearts, O Lord, that we who have known the incarnation of your Son Jesus Christ, announced by an angel to the Virgin Mary, may by his cross and passion be brought to the glory of his resurrection; who lives and reigns with you, in the unity of the Holy Spirit, one God, now and for ever. Amen.

The Visitation May 31
Father in heaven, by your grace the virgin mother of your incarnate Son was blessed in bearing him, but still more blessed in keeping your word: Grant us who honor the exaltation of her lowliness to follow the example of her devotion to your will; through Jesus Christ our Lord, who lives and reigns with you and the Holy Spirit, one God, for ever and ever. Amen.

Saint Mary the Virgin August 15
O God, you have taken to yourself the blessed Virgin Mary, mother of your incarnate Son: Grant that we, who have been redeemed by his blood, may share with her the glory of your eternal kingdom; through Jesus Christ our Lord, who lives and reigns with you, in the unity of the Holy Spirit, one God, now and for ever. Amen.

Traditional Christmas Hymns
"Lo, How a Rose E'er Blooming"

Lo, how a Rose e'er blooming
From tender stem has sprung!
Of Jesse's lineage coming
As those of old have sung.
It came, a floweret bright,
Amid the cold of winter,
When half-spent was the night.

Isaiah 'twas foretold it,
The Rose I have in mind,
With Mary we behold it,
The Virgin Mother kind.
To show God's love aright,
She bore to us a Savior,
When half-spent was the night.

This Flower whose fragrance tender
With sweetness fills the air,
Dispels with glorious splendor
The darkness everywhere.
True Man, yet very God,
From sin and death he saves us
And lightens every load.

"What Child is this"

What child is this who, laid to rest
On Mary's lap is sleeping?
Whom angels greet with anthems sweet,
While shepherds watch are keeping?
This, this is Christ the King,
Whom shepherds guard and angels sing;
Haste, haste, to bring Him laud,
The Babe, the Son of Mary.

Why lies He in such mean estate,
Where ox and ass are feeding?
Good Christians, fear, for sinners here
The silent Word is pleading.
Nails, spear shall pierce Him through,
The cross be borne for me, for you.
Hail, hail the Word made flesh,
The Babe, the Son of Mary.

So bring Him incense, gold and myrrh,
Come peasant, king to own Him;
The King of kings salvation brings,
Let loving hearts enthrone Him.
Raise, raise a song on high,
The virgin sings her lullaby.
Joy, joy for Christ is born,
The Babe, the Son of Mary.

Bibliography

L. Gambero, *Mary and the Fathers of the Church: The Blessed Virgin Mary in Patristic Thought* (San Francisco: Ignatius, 1999), and *Mary in the Middle Ages: The Blessed Virgin Mary in the Thought of Medieval Latin Theologians* (San Francisco: Ignatius, 2005). A scholarly sketch of the primary evidence so one can read the history of how the theology of Mary has developed.

B.R. Gaventa, C.L. Rigby, eds., *Blessed One: Protestant Perspectives on Mary* (Louisville, KY: Westminster John Knox, 2002). A collection of scholarly and insightful articles.

S. Hahn, *Hail, Holy Queen: The Mother of God in the Word of God* (New York: Doubleday, 2001). Roman Catholic, readable survey of major themes about Mary.

D. Longenecker, D. Gustafson, *Mary: A Catholic-Evangelical Debate* (Grand Rapids, MI: Brazos, 2003). An enjoyable toe-to-toe conversation between a Roman Catholic convert and an evangelical lawyer.

K. Norris, *Meditations on Mary* (New York: Viking Studio, 1999). This well-known Protestant writer makes use of Christian art for her meditative reflections.

J. Pelikan, *Mary through the Centuries: Her Place in the History of Culture* (New Haven: Yale University Press, 1996). The most important survey of the ongoing development of Mary in the Church.

T. Perry, *Mary for Evangelicals: Toward an Understanding of the Mother of our* LORD (Downers Grove, IL: IVP, 2006). An evangelical theologian explores a theology of Mary and finds much in the development consistent with his own evangelical faith.

J. Sweeney, *Strange Heaven: The Virgin Mary as Woman, Mother, Disciple, and Advocate* (Brewster, MA: Paraclete Press, 2006). A series of ruminations about Mary, with an abundance of suggestive quotations.

D. F. Wright, ed., *Chosen by God: Mary in Evangelical Perspective* (London: Marshall Pickering, 1989). A collection of essays about controversial topics in the discussion between Protestants and Roman Catholics.

Sources

Epigraph

John Gwili Jenkins, "Wales and the Virgin Mary," taken from Timothy George, in *Mary Mother of God*, ed. C.E. Braaten, R.W. Jenson (Grand Rapids, MI: Eerdmans, 2004), 122. The lines from "The Journey of the Magi," in *T.S. Eliot: Collected Poems, 1909-1962* (New York: Harcourt Brace & Co., 1991), 100.

Chapter 1

I borrow the Rohrschach image from Harvey Cox, the well-known liberal Harvard theologian, in his book *When Jesus Came to Harvard: Making Moral Choices Today* (Boston: Houghton Mifflin, 2004), 63.

On Nora O. Lozana-Diaz, see *Blessed Mary: Protestant Perspectives on Mary*, ed. B.R. Gaventa, C.L. Rigby (Louisville: Westminster John Knox, 2002), 90-94.

On Mark Roberts, see his blog called "The Protestant Mary?" at http://www.markdroberts.com/htmfiles/resources/protestantmary.htm #mar2705.

Chapter 2

On Martin Luther, "The Magnificat," in *Luther's Works*, ed. J. Pelikan (St. Louis: Concordia, 1956), volume 21, p. 329.

Chapter 3

On Guatemala, see Kathleen Norris, *Meditations on Mary* (New York: Viking Studio, 1999), 14.

Chapter 4

On Lynne Hybels, see *Nice Girls Don't Change the World* (Grand Rapids, MI: Zondervan, 2005).

Chapter 5

On Tacitus, see *Annals* 14.22.

Chapter 6

On Catherine Clark Kroeger, see the *IVP Women's Bible Commentary*, ed. C.C. Kroeger, M.J. Evans (Downers Grove, IL: IVP, 2002), 567.

Chapter 7

On the common Jewish expectation, see the Dead Sea Scrolls text called 4Q161, fragments 8-10.

Chapter 8

On the scholar of Greek grammar, see N. Turner, *Grammatical Insights into the New Testament* (Edinburgh: T & T Clark, 1965), 47.

Chapter 9

On Psalms of Solomon, see *Psalms of Solomon*, ch. 17. I use the translation of R.B. Wright from *The Old Testament Pseudepigrapha*, ed. J. Charlesworth (Garden City, NJ: Doubleday, 1985), volume 2. For The Infancy Gospel of Thomas, I have used the edition from J.K. Elliott, *The Apocryphal New Testament* (Oxford: Clarendon, 1993), 68-83.

Chapter 11

On Protestant leaders, see Martin Luther, *Martin Luther's Works*, ed. J. Pelikan (St. Louis: Concordia, n.d.), 11. 319-320; John Calvin, *Matthew, Mark and Luke* (Grand Rapids, MI: Eerdmans, 1989), 2. 136; J. Wesley, "An Olive Branch to the Romans," in *John Wesley*, ed. A.C. Outler (New York: Oxford, 1964), 495.

Chapter 12

On Jaroslav Pelikan, the subtitle is *Her Place in the History of Culture* (New Haven: Yale University Press, 1996).

On Howard Marshall, see *Chosen by God: Mary in Evangelical Perspective*, ed. D.F. Wright (London: Marshall Morgan and Scott, 1989), 63. On Tim Perry, see *Mary for Evangelicals: Toward an Understanding of the Mother of our* LORD (Downers Grove, IL: IVP, 2006).

On Ben Witherington, III, see *What Have They Done With Jesus? Beyond Strange Theories and Bad History* (San Francisco: HarperSanFrancisco, 2006), 118.

On the Catholic Encyclopedia, the quotations come from *The Catholic Encyclopedia* at http://www.newadvent.org/cathen/15464b.htm, and *Catechism of the Catholic Church* (New York: Doubleday, 1997), #411.

On Augustine, see Augustine, *On Nature and Grace* (Nicene and Post-Nicene Fathers, 1st series; vol. 5; Grand Rapids, MI: Eerdmans, 1971), p. 135, paragraph 42.

On Ignatius to Athanasius, see Tim Perry's discussion in *Mary for Evangelicals: Toward an Understanding of the Mother of our* LORD (Downers Grove, IL.: IVP, 2006), 146.

On Irenaeus, see Irenaeus, *Against Heresies*, from *Ante-Nicene Fathers*, vol. 1 (Grand Rapids, MI: Eerdmans, 1979), p. 455; Book 3.22.4.

On Origen, see his *Commentary on John* 1:4 and *Commentary on Matthew* 10:17; citations taken from L. Gambero, *Mary and the Fathers of the Church: The Blessed Virgin Mary in Patristic Thought* (San Francisco: Ignatius, 1999), 75-76.

Chapter 13

On Julian Charley, see *Chosen by God: Mary in Evangelical Perspective* (ed. D.F. Wright; London: Marshall Morgan and Scott, 1989), 207.

On Pope Pius IX, see http://www.newadvent.org/library/docs _pi09id.htm.

On John of Damascus, see http://www.catholicity.com/encyclopedia/ a/assumption,feast_of.html.

On Pope Pius XII, see http://www.papalencyclicals.net/Pius12/P12MUNIF.HTM, #44.

On Scott Hahn, see *Hail, Holy Queen: The Mother of God in the Word of God* (New York: Doubleday, 2001), 126.

On Pope John Paul II: His book includes his Encyclical called "Mother of the Redeemer" (*Redemptoris Mater*) with an introduction by Joseph Cardinal Ratzinger, now Pope Benedict XVI, and a commentary by the theologian Hans Urs van Balthasar. It was published in San Francisco by Ignatius Press (1988). The citation is from page 89.

On Epiphanius, see *Against Heresies* 79.9 (from Gambero, *Mary*, 128).

On Jon Sweeney, see *Strange Heaven: The Virgin Mary as Woman, Mother, Disciple, and Advocate* (Brewster, MA: Paraclete Press, 2006), 97.

On Pope Pius IX, see See http://www.ewtn.com/library/encyc/p9ubipr2.htm.

On Vatican II, see *Lumen Gentium*, par. 67.

On Athanasius, see Gambero, *Mary*, 106.

Chapter 14

On John Gwili Jenkins, I found his poem in Timothy George, in *Mary Mother of God*, ed. C.E. Braaten, R.W. Jenson (Grand Rapids, MI: Eerdmans, 2004), 122.

On G.A. Studdert Kennedy, again see Timothy George, in *Mary Mother of God*, 121.

On Nancy Duff, see *Blessed Mary: Protestant Perspectives on Mary*, ed. B.R. Gaventa, C.L. Rigby (Louisville, KY: Westminster John Knox, 2002), 65, 66.

On Tim Perry, see *Mary for Evangelicals: Toward an Understanding of the Mother of our* LORD (Downers Grove, IL: IVP, 2006), 93.

On Kathleen Norris, see *Blessed Mary: Protestant Perspectives on Mary*, ed. B.R. Gaventa, C.L. Rigby (Louisville, KY: Westminster John Knox, 2002), x.

After Words

Paraclete Press, guided by the good hands of Pamela Jordan, went out of its way for this book, and I cannot thank them enough. I must mention especially Carol Showalter, whose tireless and enthusiastic support for me reminds me why the Church is what it is. Lil Copan, my wonderful editor who believes every word of every sentence of every paragraph could perhaps be better, has become a mentor of sensible, aesthetic prose. She knows how much I appreciate her.

Several friends have read drafts of this book, and I wish here to record my gratitude for their comments: John Frye, Renee Dinges, Trevin Wax, and my sister-in-law, Pat Arnet.

Above all, I express my love to Kris. Every author needs an audience, and I have the best one on earth.

About Paraclete Press

Who We Are

Paraclete Press is an ecumenical publisher of books and recordings on Christian spirituality. Our publishing represents a full expression of Christian belief and practice—from Catholic to Evangelical, from Protestant to Orthodox.

Paraclete Press is the publishing arm of the Community of Jesus, an ecumenical monastic community in the Benedictine tradition. As such, we are uniquely positioned in the marketplace without connection to a large corporation and with informal relationships to many branches and denominations of faith.

We like it best when people buy our books from booksellers, our partners in successfully reaching as wide an audience as possible.

What We Are Doing
Books

Paraclete Press publishes books that show the richness and depth of what it means to be Christian. Although Benedictine spirituality is at the heart of all that we do, we publish books that reflect the Christian experience across many cultures, time periods, and houses of worship.

We publish books that nourish the vibrant life of the church and its people— books about spiritual practice, formation, history, ideas, and customs.

We have several different series of books within Paraclete Press, including the bestselling Living Library series of modernized classic texts; A Voice from the Monastery—giving voice to men and women monastics about what it means to live a spiritual life today; award-winning literary faith fiction; and books that explore Judaism and Islam and discover how these faiths inform Christian thought and practice.

Recordings

From Gregorian chant to contemporary American choral works, our music recordings celebrate the richness of sacred choral music through the centuries. Paraclete is proud to distribute the recordings of the internationally acclaimed choir Gloriæ Dei Cantores, who have been praised for their "rapt and fathomless spiritual intensity" by *American Record Guide*, and the Gloriæ Dei Cantores Schola, which specializes in the study and performance of Gregorian chant. Paraclete is also the exclusive North American distributor of the recordings of the Monastic Choir of St. Peter's Abbey in Solesmes, France, long considered to be a leading authority on Gregorian chant performance.

Learn more about us at our website:
www.paracletepress.com, or call us toll-free at
1-800-451-5006.

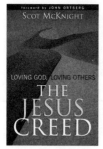
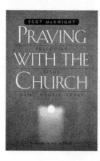